Just Another One

DC Rivera

2

CHAPTER ONE

Tues, Nov. 24, 2015

Slam! Slam! Slam! The noise penetrated the Sophomore Social Science class, interrupting Mrs. Petrakowski's explanation of the French Revolution. With Thanksgiving break within grasp, students' eyes glazed over, lost in daydreams of turkey and pumpkin pie.

The seniors were at it again, knocking over the trashcans in the hallways. To deter these antics, the school had swapped out the noisy metal bins with heavy-duty plastic ones, but they still tumbled easily, leaving a mess of trash scattered over the worn, ugly brown linoleum. Students casually booted the debris aside while chatting with friends or checking their phones. Fed up with the property damage, Manatee High replaced the garbage cans with tamper-resistant ones, featuring concrete bases and shiny steel dome lids. Despite security measures, the hooligans removed the bolted steel lids using tools stolen from Dolan's Auto Body Shop (or so the gossip claimed). Janitor Bates was the only one who should have had a master device for accessing these expensive bins.

Rumors circulated that the boys had been loosening the bolts during home room announcements. Then, around one in the afternoon when everyone was groggy from lunch and their teachers droning away, the varsity football players or soccer team boys would trudge up from the field. Some boys in class would fake being sick or plead to go to the bathroom, and they would then invade whatever hallway they had targeted for the day. And then pop, pop, pop, the steel trashcan lids went flying. The Bang! Bang! Bang! echoed down the hall, scaring the living daylights out of everyone in the adjacent classrooms. Some boys punted the lids down the hallway like soda cans; others sailed the lids like they were frisbees, hurtling against walls or doors.

Ignoring the crackling, outdated intercom system that was malfunctioning most of the time, Mrs. Petrakowski opted to grab her cell phone instead. Only teachers could have them in full view; students were required to stick theirs in backpacks, unless they sneaked them under their desks, risking a look when voice mails/texts vibrated against their crotch.

"Mr. Ziglione? Mrs. Petrakowski here. Someone is vandalizing the garbage cans again next to the Social Science room. Yes. Thank you."

Mrs. Petrakowski had faith. She relaxed somewhat.

Assistant Vice-Principal Ziglione would be on it, but the juvenile delinquents would be vamoosed by the time he hot footed from 'A' wing where the administrative offices were, to 'C' wing where the Social Sciences, Spanish and French, and Math Lab were located.

The culprits' evaded capture despite surveillance cameras, dressed identically in black masks and jeans and a school aqua windbreaker bearing the Manatee High School boldfaced across the back, and twin "sea cows" on the right and left chest pockets.

Some students whispered in hushed tones, speculating that star athletes might be responsible. If caught, they believed the athletes' status would grant them leniency.

Britney's ears pricked up as her fellow students shared their theories, wondering instead if it were bad boys/riffraff since they'd earned a reputation with suspensions, demerits, and minor arrests. Britney kept her mouth sealed about the troublemakers, concealing her inside information about the true offenders.

As Mrs. Petrakowski continued the lesson, the classroom door burst open. The teacher pivoted, the words, "then Marie Antoinette was executed in 1793" on her lips when her head exploded.

Brain matter and blood blew all over the students in the front row. The hooded, masked assailant pointed the weapon at them.

"Don't even think about going for them," the intruder warned, causing every student to glance nervously at their backpacks hanging on the hooks along the side wall, their cell phones nestled inside.

Some students screamed, while others whimpered, but everyone froze in their seats.

Britney's eyes flew to Jes's empty desk. She'd been feeling poorly the past few days and had gone to the bathroom before the slam, slam, slam began. Britney understood that Jes would escape the danger, but many others would not be so lucky.

"Some of you won't make it today," the gunman said, and a few of the girls began weeping. "Shut up or I'll know who's next. Some of you will be allowed to leave. Don't count your blessings. It'll come with a price." He drew a bead on the twenty-five students quivering in front of him. No, twenty-four, Britney thought. Jes is out of the line of fire.

A student named Lyle lunged for Mrs. Petrakowski's phone, which had clattered behind her podium. Lyle, a soccer team star, executed a dive that would surely racked up points for his team on the field. He jerked the teacher's body from the surface of her desk, cowering behind its cover as he punched in 9-1-1, but he was exterminated before he could answer the dispatcher's question of "Emergency Services. Do you need fire, police, or an ambulance?" Crimson streamed from under Lyle's body as he obnoxiously flopped between Mrs. Petrakowski's legs, pelvis-to-pelvis. It resembled a scene of intense passion, as if they were caught in flagrante delicto, playing out a fantasy inspired by Van Halen's 'Hot for Teacher.'

More kids screamed and bawled.

Britney scrutinized the gunman, analyzing his physique and posture. He appeared to resemble a wrestler from the team or simply a random stranger typifying the role of a potential shooter. Disguising his voice, though poorly, with a feeble imitation of Sylvester Stallone, his words slurred out. While his face remained masked, his eyes remained exposed. Britney's amber eyes delved into the depths of the assailant, and then, with the finesse of an accomplished actor, she unleashed a cry, delivering histrionic lines, "Oh, my God! I can't believe you're doing this! Please, don't shoot anyone else!"

"Shut up!" the gunman said: "You're next."

Britney said. "You know you won't. But you're not gonna make it out of here."

"Then neither are they," the masked intruder said, and a few seconds later, the students wailed when they heard more gunfire somewhere else in the building, foiling Britney's scenario of talking the armed intruder down or actions to aid her escape.

The realization struck Britney deeply. There was not just one assailant, but several individuals involved. Then what happened next would forever haunt her.

CHAPTER TWO

2014, Fifteen Months before the shooting

Cassie Cronrad was an easy target among her peers. Her flaming orange hair didn't resemble a trendy autumn shade or the cool ginger locks of celebrities like Bonnie Wright, Ed Sheeran, or Benedict Cumberbatch. Cassie carried a doughy inner tube of flesh around her hips and stomach, and millions of freckles dotted her face. Living in Florida only added to her challenges, as the humidity frizzed her hair into something mirroring a cross between Ronald McDonald's red afro and Carrot Top's orange coiled blowout. Then, add in the sun's mission to scorch her sensitive skin. Her complexion ranged from ivory to red, depending on whether she could hide during P.E. (by standing on the toilet seat so nobody could detect her feet, and hugging her pale arms under the fluorescent lights at Manatee High, casting a sickly green tinge across her cheeks), or had to endure torturous laps around the track or dodge ball on the field under the blazing sun.

Cassie's appearance was far from that of a CoverGirl. Her schnoz had a Roman quality, reminiscent of Rossy de Palma, though lacking the actress/model's classy Modigliani-esque nose. While sharing the same quality, Cassie was no Kate Middleton, lacking the Duchess's skinny-lipped

regalness. Curiously, Cassie's eyes boasted a lovely shade of seafoam green, deeper than even Harry Styles' ocean-like, spumy virescent eyes. Unfortunately, her lashes glowed orange like her hair, and attempts to enhance them with makeup resulted in an odd wide-eyed look, as if "over-Botoxed." Any of Cassie's features would have been reason for her to be picked on. However, when combined, her flaws created a school loser's quadlet—overweight, not pretty, and peculiar hair and skin.

Cassie's friend, Jes Marcos, fared slightly better. Like Cassie, she shared the red hair and pale skin traits. However, Jes's rich auburn hair tumbled in glossy sheets over her creamy shoulders (more radiant than The Twilight Saga actress Ashley Greene's). Her flawless complexion glistened like pearls. Unfortunately, Jes's port-wine stain birthmark marred her face, spreading from her temple to her left cheek and jawline, making her a target for bullying, along with a crushed left arm from a childhood accident. Moreover, her unique name, Jesamean, which her mom had given her simply because she liked the sound of it, further set her apart. People often butchered it, pronouncing it 'JesaMINE,' JesaMEN,' 'JEZmen,' and the worst, instead of 'Jes,' calling her 'Jism,' which so disgusted Cassie to no end. Some mistakenly assumed 'Jes' was short for 'Jessica' or called her 'Jasmine' instead, which would have been a great improvement over her actual name.

Cassie and Jes's other best friend, Britney Glascier stood tall like Gwendoline Christie from Game of Thrones, but ganglier. Britney's arms, long like a Gibbons ape, dangled just above her knees, spurring queries whether she was inflicted with Marfan syndrome (she wasn't), and fit the assumption when also noting her super skinny frame (think Antonia Campbell-Hughes from 3096 Days). Her eyes were stunning, amber like Acacia honey, but hidden behind her thick, Coke-bottle glasses. Britney's teeth were a mess (much like musician Shane MacGowan but to the nth degree), with some protruding and others sinking in. She faced daily teasing about her bony body, bug eyes, and horrible teeth.

The three of them--Cassie, Jes, and Britney—had been thrown together in sixth grade at the loser's table in the cafeteria at De Sota Middle School. It was a place where kids who weren't allowed to join the table of the school royalty - the cheerleaders, the wealthy kids, the beautiful people, the Blonde Squad, and star athletes—were seated. Alongside Cassie, Jes, and Britney were other outcasts, including: "Pizza Face," whose severe zits made it difficult to look at him; the "Finger Vampire," a weird girl with greasy hair who chewed at her cuticles and ignored her food; and "The Aliens," unattractive identical twins who communicated only with each other in their made-up language.

They were all seated together because of the school's stupid rule that required everyone to go to the cafeteria during their assigned lunch slot and stick a rump in a seat, except when retrieving food or disposing of trays. However, the Lunch Posse, a group of terrorists who wilded during lunchtime stealing food off other loser kid's plates and subjecting them to insults and general run-of-the-mill bullying comments ("Hey Loser! What's up, Fatty?"), seemed to be exempt from the rules.

Cassie couldn't recall who initiated the conversation, but she remembered how the three friends started scooting closer to each other every day, gradually moving from their initial positions at the table. Cassie, Jes, and Britney became three peas in a pod. As they prepared to enter high school, the girls looked forward to a fresh start, leaving the bullies behind. That summer before ninth grade, Britney transfigured. She filled out in all the right places, no longer resembling a stick figure or chicken legs. She became gracefully elegant, much like an Arabian horse, leaving behind her coltishness.

While Britney presented like a Victoria's Secret Angel, like a Lily Aldridge, but with amber eyes, strutting like she was built for the runway, Cassie and Jes's self-consciousness peaked, the idea of them sunbathing in a thong and teeny top like Britney, as remote as mounting a bucking bronco (Cassie with her cellulite paunches and Jes with her feelings of inadequacy). Britney got all her model poses down, displaying that banging body in microkini's that seemed glued on. She was no longer satisfied just hanging out at Cassie's pool anymore; she wanted to dazzle down at the local beach, or the bubbling springs, or tubing down the river. Cassie and Jes didn't begrudge Britney her newfound confidence and smoking body. They just didn't possess her figure and weren't about to expose their imperfections. They didn't mind accompanying Britney on her shopping excursions, (her new addiction despite limited funds), now that she had the physique to show off nice clothes. It was during one of these shopping events that the three girls noticed one of the Blonde Squaders staring at them.

Cassie groaned and whispered to her friends: "Oh no, Mean Girl at six o'clock!" They swiftly changed direction from over by the seventy per cent off sales racks, but Paloma called out, "Hey!" The three girls halted, unsure what they would encounter. Paloma, a member of the elite Blonde Squad, known for their beauty and popularity, did not speak to girls like Cassie, Jes, and Britney.

"What could she want?" Jes hissed, always on guard from past experiences of being bullied.

Another Blonde Squad girl had joined Paloma, exiting the dressing room with a bundle of expensive, fancy dresses. Both blondes loved doing pageants and owned dozens of glittering, beautiful dresses.

"Britney?" Paloma squealed. "Britney! It is you! See Tishy, I told you it was her."

Tish nodded, bored already, but her eyes, sharp as her cheek bones, did a sweep. "Britney, what have you done to yourself? I mean, your body looks amazing!" Paloma gushed.

"How did you do it? The Paleo or DASH diet? Ramp up your work out, get plastic surgery?" Tish asked, her tone dripping equal admiration and jealousy.

Britney shrugged, flattered and nervous. "I finally grew into myself, you know, just everything finally worked together, my height, my thin legs."

"Now, if you could just have the face to match the body, that would pull it all together," Paloma said.

Oh, snap. Britney deflated. Cassie's tone, all ice. "Excuse me?!"

"Don't act like you don't know what I'm talking about, you of all people," Paloma said to Cassie. "Like you wouldn't trade it all to have your friend's body. Now she needs to put it with the right face."

"Listen, you can't come up to us in a public place and start being rude —" Jes started but Britney interrupted: "No. Wait. I wanna hear what she has to say."

Paloma grinned. "See? You have possibilities, options. You get rid of those glasses, fix your teeth...well, you could be quite cute."

"Maybe if we all dyed our hair blonde, we could even be in your group," Jes snarked.

As expected, both Blonde Squad girls tittered. "Could never happen. We're all natural blondes," Tish said.

Right. Cassie rolled her eyes at Jes.

"But I can't see without my glasses. And my folks

can't afford the dental surgery I would need," Britney said.

"Tish, doesn't your dad's current wife's cousin work for a dentist?"

Tish muttered an affirmative and Paloma continued: "Okay, then, you can ask about getting Britney a discount, right?"

Tish nodded but was less than thrilled at having been enlisted for this task.

"Perfect. And my uncle has a practice in Orlando. He's an optometrist, or ophthalmologist, or something like that. I could ask him to take a look at you."

"And you're doing all this because…? The kindness of your heart? Your Christian charity?" Cassie asked.

Paloma laughed. "Of course."

Sure. There was a motive. Cassie and Jes just didn't know exactly what that was. Blonde Squad girls were all about themselves. Me. Me. Me.

Britney glowed. "That would be awesome. Thank you for your help."

"No problem. Give me your number and I'll text you later about all the deets," Paloma commanded, and Britney spit it out and Paloma entered it into her contacts on her phone. Paloma acted like she was a hero, like she was giving Britney a kidney or something. Britney lit up. Her number was now in Paloma's phone, a Blonde Squad girl!

Cassie shot Britney a look. Hey, it wasn't like she put you on speed dial, Cassie thought.

"Guess we'll see you at Manatee High at Orientation?" Paloma addressed both Cassie and Jes.

"Yes." Great. Blonde Squad girls would be following them to yet another school where they wouldn't talk to them, acknowledge, look at them.

As if to affirm this, Paloma and Tish had already dismissed them, their backs on view as they carted their dresses to the register. The blondes had their heads together, giggling, and whispering.

"You're going to do this? Accept help from them?" Cassie hissed to Britney.

"Don't judge me. This is a chance I might never get again," Britney said coolly.

Cassie said, "At what price, Brit? Would you sell your soul to Satan?"

"Yeah, well last I heard, the Devil wears Prada, so it doesn't sound like such a bad deal."

Cassie snorted and Jes shook her head.

"You understand that the Blonde Squad girls are snotty manipulators who look down on everyone except their own?" Jes said to Britney.

"They're trying to be nice to me."

"But for how long?! They're the enemy! Frenemies at best."

"Popular frenemies. Beautiful and popular. For just once in my life, I wanna be beautiful and popular too. You both would if you had the opportunity."

"Not every opportunity is a good one," Cassie said.

"Better than no opportunity at all," Britney shot back

turning her back on her friends in much the same way the Blonde Squad had, and Cassie threw a glance at Jes, both thinking that in a just a few minutes of breathing the same air as Blonde Squad girls, and Britney was already acting like them.

"Come on," Jes said, looping her arm through Cassie's as they watched Britney pay for her purchases. "She'll be okay. Let's go back to my house. I TiVo'd 'The Walking Dead.'"

Cassie, Jes, and Britney lounged at Jes's house, watching TV and munching popcorn. Britney's phone alerted her to a text, and she furrowed her brows, catching her friends' attention. The message intrigued her, as only her mom, Cassie, and Jes usually texted her. She shrieked. "OMG, it's Paloma! She's got me an appointment with both a dentist and an eye doctor! I can't believe this! So fast! And just like she said she would!"

"Yeah? And how much is all that gonna cost?" Cassie asked.

"She said for free! It's not gonna cost me a thing!"

"Brit, nothing is for free. Trust me, a Blonde Squader don't do anything unless there's something in it for them!"

"Thanks for ruining it. Thanks for your support." Britney removed her glasses and swiped her eyes.
"I'm sorry, Britney," Jes said, "But Cass is right. You absolutely know that we LYLAS (Love You Like a Sister). But think about this. Why is Paloma doing this?"

"Exactly. She's classic Massie Block, from The Clique. She heads up her own The Pretty Committee, so what's in it for her?" Cassie said.

"She sees that I have a need."

Cassie and Jes exchanged knowing looks, and Cassie said, "Paloma is only concerned about her own needs. There's a reason she's doing this, exactly what, I don't know."

"It's starting to sound very She's All That," Jes pointed out. "You, know, maybe she's trying to turn you into Laney, into a Prom Queen."

"No, Paloma wants to be the only Prom Queen," Cassie said. "But you're on the right track. She wants to make Britney her pet project. She's grooming you, but for exactly what, I dunno."

"It's very Mean Girls. Think about it. Paloma is a Blonde Squader, much like being one of the Plastics. She's a Queen Bee. She's an A-lister. She's taking Britney in and trying to mold her. You're Lindsay Lohan. Paloma is gonna make you like her."

"You mean I'm gonna start taking drugs, keep ditching rehab, and keep going to jail over and over?" Britney said, her lips crinkling.

"You know what I mean. Lindsay Lohan's character Cady. Paloma looks at you as being Cady, wants you to be in the same league."

"I'd rather you transform into Tamara," Jes grinned.

"Better yet Carrie," Cassie smiled. "Carrie 1976, that is."

"No, definitely Carrie 2013," Jes corrected.

Both turned and eyed Britney, drawing her into the debate.

"Both," Britney said. "Original Carrie, very scary. Remake Carrie, much sexier."

All three girls were huge movie buffs, particularly movies about the unpopular, picked-on girl who triumphs. Their interest in themes and cult movies, especially all things 1980s, 1990s, and of course, early Millennium, was in part due to Britney's mom, Serena, who at 31 years old, was still a "young" mom compared to some of the other moms of teens that Britney knew. Serena had introduced the trio to some great bullied-girls-ugly-girls-persevere-in-the-end movies. Serena was born just a few years after her favorite Britney Spears; therefore, Serena named her daughter after her pop-princess (something Britney couldn't decide if she hated or thought was cool).

The trio's interest in cult classics and movies about outcasts, ironically, emphasized their own status (or rather lack of status) among their peers; most of the girls' classmates had never even heard of Heathers, Clueless, and Jawbreaker; at best, some would know about Napoleon Dynamite. Whenever Cassie had mentioned these movies around some of the other girls, all she got were blank stares and crickets. This was just one more thing to separate Cassie, Britney, and Jes from their peers.

"Don't you think you should at least look these doctors up on Google and find out if they're legit?

Are they at least on Facebook? I mean, I wouldn't solely rely on Paloma's word! Look at her! She's only fourteen, and I think she's already had Botox!" Cassie said.

"No, that tight, high-end look is natural," Britney quipped. "Anyway, I'm on it." She had already pulled up some information on her iPhone. "Wow, these doctors got 4.8-5.00 stars on their reviews! They're quality! Paloma was right, I gotta give it to her."

Britney's text alerted her, and she read it and squawked, startling her friends.

"That better be because Chris Hemsworth asked you out," Cassie said.

"I'm certain he's married," Jes said, Cassie rolling her eyes.

"Paloma and Tish want to go with me to Orlando for both my eye and dental surgery! I don't know which one would be first, but get this, Paloma's dad said he'd get us a limo!"

Cassie and Jes' mouths fell open. Then Cassie said, "That would be perfect, Brit. Leave your mom home, you go to some stranger's office to get your teeth fixed, and you ride back with these hyenas chattering the whole time and you're all swollen up and hurting and not able to talk? That sounds like a great time."

"No, they give you good drugs at the dentist office. You saw YouTube Jack after he had his wisdom teeth pulled. I'll be like that. I'll be out of it."

"That'll be awesome. Those stupid Blonde Squaders will probably post your picture on

Snapchat, you drooling all over yourself." Cassie snickered.

"They're not gonna do that," Britney said.

"And you know this because...?" Cassie asked.

"Why would they go to all this trouble and then do that?"

"Exactly, Britney! They're going to a lot of trouble helping you. What is the motivation? What's in it for them?" Jes said.

"What if they really are just trying to be nice?"

Both Cassie and Jes broke out into hysterical laughter. "Stop, I'm gonna bust something from laughing so hard. LMBO," Jes said.

"Y'all ever read this science fiction book called Uglies? It's about everybody being unattractive, but when they get to be sixteen, they're automatically eligible for cosmetic surgery to turn them into being pretty. Because that's what everyone wants, right?" Cassie cut her eyes to Britney, who didn't answer, but folded her arms across her chest. Cassie continued, "But some citizens in the dystopian society see that there can be downsides to suddenly being beautiful, like just being accepted because of outward appearances only. Some of the uglies reject this imposed standard. They rebel because they see conformity as being BS, and who the pretties really are."

"Fascinating," Britney said, then more coolly, "I'm still going with Tish and Paloma." Then perusing an incoming text, she clarified: "My eye consultation is in one week. And if all goes well, my surgery is two weeks after that. My dental consultation is in three weeks, and then surgery if my doctor says I'm good to go."

"And your mom has signed off on this?" Jes asked.

"Not exactly. Gotta wait for the right moment to spring it on her."

"That should go well," Jes snorted.

"I don't see the problem. They're offering to pay for everything!"

"The first thing your mom is gonna say is, why would they do that? Then what will you tell her?"

"That they're my new, rich, generous friends?" Britney said

"Your mother is gonna think it's sketchy. We think it's sketchy."

"My mother will be thrilled that as a single mom she won't have to pay for it, won't have to beg my wayward father for money, and that I'm gonna be happy."

Cassie wasn't convinced. She threw a look at Jes, who seemed as dubious as she was.

Serena, Britney's mom, had many questions about this whole business, peppering Britney hard about who, what, when, where, and why's, burning up the phone lines with all the back and forth between the doctor's offices, Paloma and Tish's folks, and all the actors involved. When Serena had been satisfied that all i's has been dotted and all t's had been crossed, then and only then had she given her approval and green lighting Britney to move ahead—one step closer to cosmetic heaven and realizing her dream of transforming into a beauty. In the end, Serena insisted on accompanying Britney for the consultations/procedures, and yes, in the limo-- despite the less than enthusiastic response received; three sullen teenagers balking at having the parental authority sharing their ride. But, hey, this was the ground rules Serena had laid down, so be it.

Cassie and Jes felt left out, which was not unfamiliar to them as bullied kids. However, this time it was different because it involved one of their own. Each girl – Britney, Cassie, Jes, was a vertex in their triangular friendship, with each line and angle connecting them. Despite feeling excluded, Cassie and Jes did not let it overshadow Britney's happiness. Britney's well-being was impossible to resent. Still, Cassie couldn't shake the feeling that something was about to change, and not just Britney's outward appearance.

"I'll keep y'all in the know about my procedures," Britney said to Cassie and Jes. "I'll shoot you a selfie when I'm out of recovery, okay?"

"Well, you better," Jes said.

"Oh, and get this, my mom actually let me buy a new outfit to wear to Orlando! And even though it's from Walmart, it's so cute, and both Tish and Paloma liked it!"

The fact that it met with the Blonde Squader's approval, made Cassie slightly nauseous. The thought of Paloma and Tish flanking Britney in the limo instead of Cassie and Jes, made Cassie want to throw up, the Blonde Squad girls with their designer clothes, perfect blonde hair and not a strand out of place, their comfortable but expensive workout shoes, their costly perfume wafting inside the limo. It was sickening. Made Cassie sick with envy, for even caring about what those stupid Blonde Squad girls did, then sick with guilt that she felt jealousy instead of being super happy about Britney's welfare, about her outcome.

Cassie knew that Britney's procedure wasn't purely cosmetic. The way Britney's teeth jutted out, they hurt her, interfered with her ability to eat or talk. Simple tasks such as brushing and flossing for her were a nightmare, all those spiky teeth going every which way. Britney's mouth reminded Cassie of a cave; stalactites on the roof of her mouth hanging down like icicles and the lower teeth popping out of her gums like stalagmites.

Britney had shared with Cassie and Jes that when she had been about nine years old that she so full of self-loathing about her eyes and teeth, that she had taken a rock and had tried to knock out her own incisors, pounding away until they cracked but did not fall out, her mouth aching and bloody from her efforts and her mother screaming when she saw. Then there was the matter of Britney's eyes. Cassie didn't know exactly what Britney's condition was, but she did know that her friend was blind without her glasses. She also knew that for some reason Britney was not a good candidate for regular contact lenses and Britney's pediatric eye doctor had recommended she wait until she was older for corrective surgery, which she never had but maybe that was all going to change now that Britney's mom had spoken to the new doctor recommended by Tish's whoever (her father's current wife's cousin or something). Britney was going to be able to chew her food normally, speak normally, not constantly hiding her mouth behind her hand. Britney's sight would be twenty-twenty, her beautiful eyes no longer hidden behind those ugly glasses. With Britney's knockout body and corrected vision and new smile, she was going to be something. Cassie just hoped by Britney becoming something, that Cassie and Jes wouldn't become less.

CHAPTER THREE

"Can you believe it?" Britney said. "I've actually thrown my glasses out! No more being called Four Eyes!"

Cassie wasn't certain about the specifics of the procedure Britney had undergone (Lasik?), but it seemed to have improved Britney's vision vastly. After her recovery, Britney would then be able to get fitted with special contact lenses (scleral) to assist her beyond the corrective surgery.

Cassie had always thought Britney's eyes, behind those thick lenses, resembled those of a tarsier, a little primate with huge amber-goldish eyes. However, Cassie kept her thoughts to herself, after all, she had her own defects.

The only remaining imperfection for Britney was her teeth, which were scheduled to be fixed the week prior to Christmas break.

"I got permission," she told her friends, "to get my assignments in advance. Then, that'll give me about two-and-a-half week's recovery period."

"But...you won't be able to eat all the good stuff during our break," Cassie pointed out.

It was tradition for the three girls to visit the sweet shops that sold Santa Clause cookies, or pumpkin spice lattes, and Reindeer cake pops.

"I know. But it's a sacrifice I'll have to make this year.

Y'all can still go. I'll probably be gumming my food like some geriatric."

"Yeah, but it won't be the same," Jes said.

It was at that moment Cassie realized when Britney returned to school in the new year, she would be a completely transformed person. She and Jes anticipated that 2015 would be the same sucky thing for them as 2014 (and the year before that, and so on).

Cassie remembered when they'd entered freshman year, and Britney's banging body and stunning eyes garnered a lot of attention. Paloma made sure everyone knew that she had suggested Britney's eye surgery and upcoming dental surgery, although she seemed to have forgotten that Tish had also been involved. Paloma stopped short of taking credit for Britney's body since it had nothing to do with her. Britney's good genes, answered prayers, structured workouts, and cleaner eating habits were responsible for her transformation.

Similar to their middle school, the new high school was ruled by a hierarchy where wealthy kids, star athletes, and the Blonde Squad reigned supreme. While ninth graders were traditionally picked on by upperclassmen, the Blonde Squaders, carryovers with their popularity from junior high, were exempt from such treatment and were even embraced by the upperclassmen cliques, clubs, and parties.

At high school, Cassie, Jes, and Britney no longer had to sit at the losers table at lunchtime. That was because there were benches alongside the wings and most days they bought their lunch and sat outside. However, the seating arrangements were still divided. The upperclassmen and Elites claimed the shady spots next to the awnings; the stoners next to the stairs where they could sneak a joint under the steps; the geeks congregated near the library benches, and the losers were relegated to the noisy area near the gym without any shade trees.

Two weeks into the new school term, the Blonde Squad had extended an invitation to Britney to join them at the shady bench next to the awnings. It became a regular Friday thing. As if they were trying her out. Like an audition. Cassie and Jes had wondered if it would become a daily thing once Britney's teeth got fixed. The first time Paloma and a sophomore named Melody had called Britney over, she'd hesitated. Cassie and Jes urged her on even though they really weren't keen about it.

"You sure?" Britney asked, and Cassie responded, "Go."

Britney, who'd learned to hide her smile from others -- usually by a palm to her mouth, stared at her two best friends, grinned widely, saying: "It's just for the day," then remembering her horrid teeth, she slammed her lips together and followed Paloma and Melody to the Elite/school royalty bench, where other Blonde Squaders mingled with upperclassmen cheerleaders, and impossibly good looking football and basketball players.

Of course, what started as a "just for the day" thing became a regular gathering. Britney attempted to include her two best friends, suggesting to Paloma and Astrid, a sophomore, on their second invitation, if Jes and Cassie could accompany her. The Blonde Squad/Elite girls cackled, then rolled their eyes, Paloma, in particular. Astrid's long fake eyelashes tangled with her eyebrows. She blinked, winked, and stuck her tongue out in an attempt to untangle them, resembling someone either drunk, stoned, or having a seizure. Eventually, Astrid managed to free the fake lashes with her long purple nails.

Once Astrid completed her carrying on, in answer to Britney's question, Paloma answered: "Them hanging out with us? Ugh, as if!" She was burning Cassie and Jes with *Clueless* quotes. Despite Britney casting a sharp glance at the girls then looking apologetically at Cassie and Jes, she followed the school royalty girls, leaving her two best friends behind.

Cassie and Jes, both movie buffs, couldn't help but to admire Paloma's dig, since many kids their own age would be…well, clueless about the classic movie. Still, it didn't feel good being a reject.

"I hope Tarantula-Eyes gets mistaken for a spider and a bird pecks out her eyeball," Jes said.

"How does Astrid even curl her lashes that high?" Cassie asked.

"At least two pairs of fakes and then piling on mascara."

"A crapload of mascara," Cassie agreed.

"I heard she spikes them like that because she wants them to pop like they're stars. You know, because 'Astrid' means star-like radiance, from 'astron.' I think it means 'divine beauty' too."

Both girls eyed Astrid. She was definitely that. She'd never be a Blonde Squader, but why would she want to? She was one of the Elites, her black hair swinging around her shoulders, her nose perfect and perky, her body curvy.

Cassie grinned. "You know what else 'Astrid' means? It's Scandinavian and a combination of Ássfriðr. That's Áss, which means 'a god,' and 'friðr' which means 'beautiful,'"

"How do you know this?"

"Googled it, of course. But you're missing the point. It's spelled 'Ássfriðr.' So, Astrid's name is Ass Frior."

"Ass Free or?"

"Yeah. She's ass free. Or."

"She's definitely not ass-free. That J-Lo booty." And both girls cracked up, their loud laughter drifting across the courtyard.

"Your friends sound like the Joker. Heath Ledger's, not Jack Nicholson's," Paloma remarked to Britney.

Britney glanced at her friends, wishing she was in on their fun. She wondered if they would fill her in later about what had been so funny. They kept looking over at Astrid, so she figured it was about Britney's new friends. She knew they must think she thought she was hot stuff hanging out with the popular girls, and she *was* flattered. But she hated feeling in the middle between the Elites and her two best friends. If the Blonde Squad and Elites would only give her friends a chance. But she knew there wasn't a snowball in Hades' chance of that happening.

Cassie and Jes surveyed Paloma, Tish, Astrid, and another half-dozen upper-Elites or Blonde Squaders gathering around Britney, their fake-laughs and expensive perfume drifting back toward the duo. "I still don't trust them," Cassie said. "I still say they've got an ulterior motive for helping Brit."

Jes, squinting at the gaggle of girls and commented: "You watch. They'll turn Britney into one of them. The Blonde Squaders will have her dying her brown hair blonde, putting on outrageous makeup, dressing fancy, and teasing her hair up."

"I haven't seen so much big hair, fake lashes, and shiny lips since my mom made me go to Glamour Shots a couple of years ago," Cassie said. She'd admit the makeover had boosted her confidence - the whole point of her mother sending her, she was so down on herself - and made her feel beautiful. Correction: she still didn't look beautiful, but she definitely looked better.

But Cassie couldn't maintain that look — she wouldn't even know where to begin with the hair fluff out with the blow dryer and mousse and spray, the gluing of eyelashes, and applying foundation and the makeup application the Glamour Shots team spackled her with, four specialists with little brushes attacking her like they were painting a faded ugly wall.

"Your photos were awesome," Jes said. "Like the After shots of contestants on *The Swan*." Secretly, Jes had dreamt of appearing on the plastic surgery makeover TV show. Unfortunately, it had been cancelled after a few seasons and before she'd ever had a chance to pitch her case. And with her port-wine stain, her medical situation would have been complicated.

"I think Paloma and Tish think that's what this is, Britney is their subject, their transformation. Paloma thinks she's Dr. Dubrow."

"No, you have to be board-certified."

Cassie squinted at her. "It was a joke, Jes. Jeez."

"I know. I'm not myself. I'm worried about Britney."

"About her dental surgery?"

"Of course." That much was true. But Jes also worried that Britney was distancing herself as her beauty became more apparent. Jes brimmed with envy. No way would she admit this. She and Cassie were maligning Paloma and Tish for transforming Britney, but in private, Jes (and maybe Cassie too) wondered why Paloma hadn't picked *them* for a makeover. To cover up her thoughts, she made light of her previous statement. "Well, Paloma might not be board-certified, but she's certifiable."

"Oh, they all are," Cassie laughed, jerking her head toward the group. Except Britney. But the longer you hung out with a group, the more likely you were to adopt their behavior. Bandwagon effect, peer pressure, group mores. Cassie didn't know where Britney fell but hoped it wouldn't be away from her and Jes.

CHAPTER FOUR

Paloma, Tish, Melody, Astrid, and an Elite named Millicent and another Blonde Squader named Ivy were hanging out at Tish's house. The girls had just returned from a huge shopping spree, and cute shorts, tops, lingerie, shoes, and purses were scattered all over Tish's king-sized bed. Everything was name brand, designer wear, and expensive. Every girl's folk had money and each of them had their own credit line at several chic boutiques and high-end shops, or their own credit card.

Tish and Melody were trading tops and slacks, they were wearing the same size, and this was normal for them. Some of the other girls were asking to borrow each other's new purses, or shorts. There was also an assortment of new makeup, lotions, and nail polish strewn across Tish's huge vanity.

Ivy scooped up some lipstick and said, "Who here wears this color?"

Tish said, "It's for Britney. Melody bought it for her."

"For what reason?" Millicent asked, holding a blouse up to her image in the mirror and scrutinizing it.

"You think she can afford this herself?" Melody asked, then to Millicent she added, "Pair that blouse with the tan shorts."

Millicent nodded at how perfect it looked together. "Explain to me again why you're helping her?"

"She's our charity case this year," Paloma said.

"Everybody likes an underdog who becomes top dog."

"It seems she's a show dog you've put a lot of money into," Ivy said, admiring a red bra and panties set she'd just purchased.

"A good show dog brings attention to the owner," Tish said.

"So, what does that mean?" Ivy asked.

"Britney is my creation," Paloma said, slipping on a new pair of heels and gazing in the full-length mirror. At Tish's sharp glance, she added, "Tishy's too. So, when people see what Britney's become, they compliment us, give *us* admiration."

"I'd say Britney's the one getting a lot of admiration," Millicent pointed out.

"Maybe. Are you jealous?" Melody said, kidding but not kidding.

"Jealous? Of course not. She's got a good body and all, but so do we. We thicc and no butterface's here ever. And we're pretty without having to have surgery done. And the girl is broke, so she'll never be able to wear quality stuff like us. But I'm not loving Britney's getting looked over by several guys I'd want for myself," Millicent said.

"Oh, come on, Milli, you're going out with three different guys right now," Tish laughed. "How many more do you want?"

"I'm just saying, she's competition."

"No, girlfriend, she coopetition."

"There's no such thing," Ivy said.

"There's most definitely such a thing. My dad would tell you it's a business strategy. It's like working together and cooperating, even if you're competing with someone. Like when Tish and I are in pageants together," Paloma said.

"So, how's coopetition helping us?" Ivy asked. "You know ninety-five per cent of the school losers would love to be one of us. And here you bring in Britney like she's earned it."

"She didn't earn it. That's what makes her our little puppet, Ivy. We pull her strings. She works for us," Melody said, grabbing her new gold clutch and pairing it with some yellow slides.

"Like leverage?" Millicent asked.

"Exactly," Tish said.

"Like a rescue dog," Melody said. "They're always so grateful to be given a chance and then they'll do whatever you tell them to."

"So that's what you're doing this for? To use Britney?" Ivy asked.

"Uuuh, yeah," Paloma rolled her eyes. "We control her. Therefore, we manipulate whatever situation we want."

"And what is it we want?" Ivy asked.

"Well, I'm sure she'll come in handy eventually. Right now, the girl is still got healing up to do after her next surgery. But by next year, she'll be metamorphosed and at our beck and call," Tish said.

"We're Alphas," Melody reminded them. "People like Britney, are our Betas."

"Precisely. I don't give to someone like her, unless I expect something back in return," Paloma said, donning her new skirt and Tish's new blouse. "As a matter of fact, I'm thinking about giving an opportunity to another loser girl. That way we take another bottom-feeder and co-op them, absorb them into school royalty and are rewarded by their devotion."

"Who's the girl gonna be?" Millicent asked.

Paloma shrugged. "Gotta finishing fixing Britney before we can scope another one."

"There's dozens of loser chicks at school," Melody said.

"Yeah, not like you gotta go hunting for them. I can think of ten right off the top of my head," Ivy said.

"You're pretty quiet over there, Astrid," Paloma noticed.

Astrid caught Paloma and the other girls' gaze in the mirror where she was experimenting with different eye shadows. "Just listening to the convos."

"And?" Tish said.

"Just remember, sometimes the rescue dog turns on its master — or mistress in this case," Astrid said, wiping the blue shadow from her eyelids.

"No way," Paloma laughed. "Britney's my peasant. And will do what I tell her to. If she knows what's good for her."

"Right. She's like her namesake," Melody smiled. "I'm A Slave 4 U," she sang.

The other girls, including Astrid joined in.

"Exactly," Paloma grinned, pleased.

CHAPTER FIVE

Britney had undergone dental surgery, which included extractions, implants, and veneers. Cassie didn't have all the details but knew Britney had issues with her cross-bite and missing teeth, requiring a procedure called a full-arch. Cassie had only heard of an arch of a foot; she had never heard of an arch in your mouth. Thinking about arches reminded Cassie of the golden arches of McDonalds and her mouth began to water.

Anyhow, everyone assumed that Britney would go from having wonky teeth to perfect teeth in no time. It turned out that it wasn't that simple. The three weeks Britney had allotted for her recovery was just the first phase.

"I feel like the time I tried to smash my teeth out with the rock," Britney told her friends.

"Well, they had to take all your teeth out, so pushing and pulling, and pounding, no wonder you're miserable," Jes said. "Then hammering, drilling, and bolting the implants in."

"Thanks for the visual on my pain," Britney said.

"Did they get a picture of your mouth when you had no teeth?" Cassie asked.

"No idea," Britney muttered.

"Because we could have posted it on Snapchat."

"Why would I want my toothless mouth on there for everyone to gawk at?"

"I bet you looked like my great aunt Edna without her dentures," Jes grinned.

"So attractive, I'm sure," Cassie said.

"And the whole thing isn't over yet," Britney winced. "I'm almost healed from the implants, but then comes the crowns, and then the porcelain veneers. I still got months ahead of me."

"Well, the worst is behind you, right? And you look better already."

"Yeah but had I known all the months of healing involved, I might have waited until the summer."

It was hard to believe it had only been the previous summer when Paloma had broached Britney about helping her with eye and dental surgery. Now, several months into 2015 and with only a few more months left of the school year, Cassie and Jes knew what their friend had said was not entirely true. Britney was afraid that if she put it off, maybe Paloma and Tish would lose interest and not help her. Plus, with her eyes already done, she felt compelled to finish her journey.

By April, Britney's transformation was complete. Her eyes popping with makeup, thanks to Paloma, Astrid, and Tish, and her smile bright and perfect, Britney went from being the Elites and Blonde Squaders Friday girl, to eating over at their bench almost every day. Her best friends wondered when she'd pull away from them entirely.

When Melody and Paloma took Britney to the best hair salon in town and approved her swingy layered haircut and blonde streaks, Cassie and Jes knew it was only a matter of time.

However, it wasn't the Elite girls or the Blonde Squaders who put the nail in the coffin to their friendship, but rather a boy.

CHAPTER SIX

Jester Ray JR Pynes, an Elite member of the Trap Shooting Squad, didn't boast the mad skills of the star basketball or football jocks, known as Ath-Elites, but was majorly popular and part of the in-crowd. Ever since his parents' split-up, his dad had graced him with a generous monthly allowance, as Pops had remarried shortly after the divorce, leaving Jester with his mom. As a junior, Jester hung out with a mixed group of upper-class Elites, school royalty, and sports guys.

As Paloma and her Squaders drew all eyes with their shiny gold manes, cleavage, and curves, Jester felt the allure of their power. He couldn't help but stare at the statuesque, beautiful girl with semi-brown hair and chunky blonde streaks.

"Who's that?" he asked, pointing.

"Paloma and Tish's Olive Penderghast," replied Chaney Smith, the captain of Manatee High's Soccer Team.

"You mean like from *Easy A*?"

"Yeah, they created her. Paid for her eye and dental surgery. Got her threads. Revamped her hair and makeup."

"Was she really all that needy before?"

"Hmm, pretty ratchet."

"She's fire," Jester said.

"Now she is. Dude, you've seen her around. You just

never noticed her before because she hadn't been completely cooked yet. Surprised though you didn't notice that body, but maybe that was because at the beginning of the school year, she was mostly just a Goodwill dumpster diver hiding her assets under bad clothes, that is until the Squaders gave her their hand-me-downs."

"Who's she going out with?"

"Nobody. I hear she ain't dating anyone," Chaney said.

"Why not?"

"Maybe she's shy."

"I'm the guy to kill the shy and bring on the shine," Jester bragged.

"Then give it a shot, man. Here she comes. Her name is Britney."

"What's up, Paloma? Tishy?" Jester greeted as they approached.

"Hi Jester. You're looking very well put together today," Paloma flirted.

"And you're on fleek as always, Paloma."

"That's sweet."

"Who's your beautiful friend?" Jester asked.

Britney blushed, and Paloma's expression briefly soured before she recovered. "Britney, meet Jester."

"I'm also called JR. Jester 'Jess' Ray."

"Jes? My best friend's name is Jes too. The other best friend is Cassie."

Paloma and her friends lost interest and turned away to talk to others.

"Well, as long as you don't get us confused when you become my shorty."

"At five feet ten, I'll never be anyone's 'shorty,'" Britney said.

Chaney chimed in, "That was a good comeback, bro."

Jester loomed over Britney, saying, "I'm six-three. You could definitely be my 'shorty'."

Britney didn't appreciate the cockiness, but oh, those eyes! Green-gray with a hint of amber - her eye color - around the pupils. Britney wondered what color their future children's eyes would be, a swirl of amber-gold and green-gray. The idea of mixing colors sparked her imagination, thinking about their bodies being intertwined. To conceal her embarrassment, she asked, "Your name is Jester, like a minstrel?"

His face scrunched up. "Menstrual?"

Britney's cheeks turned as red as blood. "No, a minstrel, an entertainer. A jester."

"You've lost me, honey. But I'm fascinated by your vocabulary and my lack of it."

"A balatro is a professional jester, or a fool."

Chaney laughed. "Dude, did she just call you an idiot?"

"You would know all about that. Can you give us some space?"

"Dipping," Chaney said, drifting away toward a group of popular girls who would appreciate his humor more.

"Sorry. I just meant, like a jokester."

"They don't call me the class clown and prankster for nothing. It means I can dish out zingers and take them too."

"I wasn't trying to insult you. I meant jesters were known for acrobatics, juggling, and magic tricks."

"I can't do a backflip or juggle, but I can work some magic with the right person, Miss Smart Girl. Wanna see all my tricks?"

Jester's green-grey eyes twinkled, and Britney was captivated. "Yeah, show me how you can transform from swaggy to mature."

He grinned, his teeth as perfect as Britney's surgically enhanced ones.

Jester couldn't tell if Britney was talking down to him or boosting him up, but she had it all – beauty, brains, and a great body. "I can handle adulting," he claimed, linking his fingers with hers. And just like that, they became a couple.

CHAPTER SEVEN

Cassie and Jes didn't hear about Britney and Jester's romance from Britney herself. Instead, they found out through Astrid, an Elite they had never even spoken to before. As they strode toward the benches, Astrid breezed by and said, "Guess y'all will be one down now, huh?"

"What?" Jes asked, unwrapping her ham sandwich.

"Your bestie."

Cassie ripped open a package of Hostess Crème-filled Twinkies with her teeth. When Astrid's double-fake-lashed eyes blinked in disapproval (or maybe it was because her lashes were stuck again, who knows?), to be mean, Cassie asked: "Wanna bite?"

Astrid shuddered as if Cassie had offered a baby's finger. Or maybe she simply didn't want to get cooties from a loser's lunch.

Jes swallowed a big chunk of ham and said, "Bestie? Like as in Britney? Yeah, we know she eats with y'all every day now. Doesn't mean we're down one. We still all hang."

"I'm sure her time for hanging with you will be at a premium now that she's got a boyfriend."

"What?" Jes mumbled, her mouth gluey with bread and meat.

"You're misinformed," Cassie said.

"And you're out of the loop, girlfriend."

Jes nearly choked on her sandwich. "Who's been

spreading these rumors?"

"No rumors. Facts. Don't y'all check your socials, hear the gossip in the hallway? Doesn't your girl keep you on the up, spill you the tea?" Astrid flipped her black hair, a smug smile as she delivered the news.

"Apparently we didn't get the memo." Cassie bit out the words, angry at Britney for not informing her and Jes, and annoyed to have to deal with this dirt-disher Elite.

"Didn't get the *memo*?!" Astrid's voice pitched. "What is this? Like the nineties? Not only are y'all out of touch, but you're also out of date! Honestly, I'd expect you two to be basic, but to not even know what your suppose-ed best friend is up to? Un-freakin'-believable!"

Cassie's face burned. She wanted to tell Astrid to stuff it, and would have, but Jes blurted: "So who's the guy?"

"Britney's boo? Jester Ray JR 'Jess/Jesse' Pynes, of course."

Jes and Cassie glanced at each other. They'd heard of him, a top rung high schooler and upperclassman.

"Well, guess you should have been told. But now you Better Ask Somebody, hmmm?" The dig was delivered to let the questioners know that they were clueless. Then, seeing Paloma, Tish, and Melody, she shouted: "Hey, wait up! You won't believe this!"

"I feel like an idiot," Jes said, having lost her appetite and sticking the rest of her soggy sandwich in a Ziploc.

"I feel betrayed," Cassie said, motioning for Jes to hand her the remainder of the sandwich. She never lost her appetite, and if anything, bad news made her want to eat even more. The Twinkies and potato chips she'd brought were nothing but crumbs after she had chowed through.

"We shouldn't just confront Britney," Jes said.

"No? I feel very confrontational." Cassie's eyes narrowed as she bit into the sandwich.

"I know. Me too. But it's not going to help. We'll have her over to watch a movie this weekend. Same thing we've been doing for years. And then we'll ask her about this guy."

"You think it's a coincidence she's going with a guy with the same name as one of her best friends?"

"I don't know if it's a coincidence or not. But it sure makes me feel less special," Jes said.

CHAPTER EIGHT

Jes, Cassie, and Britney sprawled on the couch at Cassie's house. Jes and Cassie shared a bowl of buttered popcorn while Britney sipped a green smoothie that her friends would no way touch. Jes's face screwed up at it and Cassie made gagging noises. Once, they used to playfully lob kettle corn at each other, giggling hysterically and not caring about the mess. However, ever since Britney got her new choppers, she avoided certain foods that could get stuck in her teeth or cause discoloration. Her friends understood, but it made their get-togethers less fun.

"Ready-Freddy?" Cassie asked, popping the movie into the DVD player.

"What did you pick?" Britney asked.

"*Picture This.*" Cassie and Jes had chosen it by design, hoping the movie's theme would help them segue into a conversation about Britney's new romance with Jester.

"We've seen it like four times," Britney pointed out, slurping the remainder of her swampy looking drink.

"Three," Jes corrected.

"We got anything else we haven't seen umpteen times?" Britney asked, crossing her shapely legs from her spot on the couch. She wore one of Paloma's castoffs, a practically brand new emerald green silk shorts that Britney couldn't help but caress, tracing the smooth material with her pink tipped fingernails.

Her matching camisole and lounging jacket pulled the ensemble all together.

Jes, on the other hand, donned old pajama bottoms with knee holes and an oversized white T-shirt featuring One Direction. Cassie sported worn-out grey sweats with pizza grease stains and a vintage T-shirt from an Alice Cooper concert she'd bought online. Both girls recollected when Britney wore her favorite black Ed Hardy T-shirt with a tiger growling across her chest and discolored grey sweatpants. Jes and Cassie felt dowdy next to the glammed-up Britney.

"We thought you'd like this one," Cassie said. "The unpopular Mandy snags the most popular guy in school. Sorta like before you were school royalty and honorary Blonde Squader. Like you getting this guy Jess/Jesse or Jester, Jester/Ray, or JR or whatever he calls himself. Seriously, does anyone need to have four names?"

Britney sighed, leaning toward the bowl as if she were going to grab a piece of popcorn, but then remembered she needed to keep her pristine teeth from getting chunks of crap stuck in them. She sat erect and said, "I wanted to tell y'all."

"And you were being held captive by kidnappers, unable to do it?" Jes asked.

"I didn't want y'all to feel bad."

"You mean worse than realizing everyone in school knew but us and that witch Astrid had to tell us?" Cassie said.

"I'm sorry. It's just…things have ended up different than what I thought they'd be."

"Like you're a bombshell now, an A-lister, with a handsome boyfriend and your ugly friends aren't in the same league?"

"Don't say that, Cassie."

"Why? Because you don't wanna hear the truth? Or you just don't know how to get out of being with your bottom rung friends?"

"Because that's not how it is."

Cassie and Jes laughed, and Britney felt the sting, but carried on. "We'll always be friends. To the end. Even to death."

"That makes me feel so much better," Jes snickered.

"You know what I mean. Nothing is going to come between the three of us."

"Not even a boy?" Cassie asked.

"Especially not a boy." But Cassie and Jes knew that it had already started. Instead of acknowledging it, Cassie said, "So tell us all about this hunk. And don't leave anything out." And the movie was temporarily forgotten as the two girls lived vicariously through their best friend.

CHAPTER NINE

Cassie and Jes didn't have their driver's licenses yet. So, of course, no car. However, Jesse did. Even though the girls initially opposed Britney having a boyfriend, they couldn't resist being carted around by a hot guy with a cool car. At first, Jester wasn't exactly keen on having Judgmental Jes and the surly Cassie around, but then he saw it as a way to gain their approval for dating Britney.

Jester's charms had melted many a girl's heart, and Cassie and Jes also thawed that late May as school ended. The girls were either resigned that Britney had a boyfriend and Jester was there to stay, or they were bowled over by Jester treating them to countless fast-food joints. Britney opted for salads and Diet Coke, while Jes teetered between healthy things and caloric laden delights. However, Cassie always stuffed her face with French fries, crispy chicken sandwiches, and shakes. Jester could swear Cassie had put on at least ten pounds since school got out, but he didn't dare ask.

By early July, he felt like he'd broken through the wall that Cassie and Jes had erected when he had first started going out with Britney. The alcohol he supplied didn't hurt, either. Whereas the three girls used to spend their weekends watching classic teen-girl-ugly-ducklings-turned-swan movies, they now hit one of the few drive-in theatres in existence in their area, where Friday night marathons included *Legally Blond, 10 Things I Hate About You, The Craft*, and *Heathers*. Although Jester's taste ran to *Die Hard*, he went along with the choices that made the chicks happy. It was pretty freaking funny, too, getting the girls sauced, and him slightly horny for Britney, unable to do much more than give her a smooch every now and then.

Before Jester corrupted them, the girls had never imbibed. "No kidding?" he'd asked. "Not even a little sneaky shot of Mommy's supply?"

"Nope," the three girls had replied. Their initial nervousness about indulging had been overridden by their alky greed. They eagerly presented their cups as Jester poured Jack, Crown, or Bacardi, whatever he could steal from his mom's liquor cabinet, though his dad's bar was obtainable.

Now, all three girls were giggling over nothing and paid no attention to the movie. Ordinarily, Jester would have been turned off to this kind of female silliness, but they were so comical that he didn't mind. Besides, alcohol acted like truth serum, making the girls spill secrets. He knew more than he probably should – details about feminine products, chicks' fantasies, and even the horror of crotch rot (fungal vaginal infections). He also knew that the three girls were on the same menstrual cycle (known as period syncing), a phenomenon disputed by science but experienced firsthand by Cassie, Britney, and Jes. With alcohol involved, every outing seemed to uncover another hush-hush Jester had learned about the three best friends.

The more Jester got to know Cassie, the less he liked her. Despite being amicable to him, he knew she was not on Team Jester and would love nothing more than for him and Britney to break up. On the other hand, the more Jester got to know Jes, the more he liked her and found they had a lot in common, perhaps even more than what he had with Britney. Jester and Jes both liked John Green books, so of course *Paper Towns* had been the movie to see that July. They were also into Charlie Puth ("Too vanilla, and not enough thug," Britney proclaimed, and Cassie playfully quipped, "Charlie who?" Her musical preferences leaned toward classic rock anthems and bands like Papa Roach and Halestorm. Whenever "See You Again" blasted from Jester's car radio that summer, he and Jes warbled at the top of their lungs, while the other friends yelled "Shush it!" And Jester kidding Britney saying, "Charlie Puth with Wiz Khalifa, now is that thug enough for you?"

Jester was surprised to learn Jes enjoyed firing guns, and following a visit to the target range, he recommended her as one of the alternates for fall term in the Trap Shooting Squad for when they returned to school. She was quite good at firing a weapon and her confidence soared after their friendly competition at the shooting range. She'd forgotten all about hiding her port wine stain with her hair, intent on hitting the bullseye.

"Ladies?" Jester said, waved the bottle of booze.

"Oh, I shouldn't," Britney remarked, her cheeks rosy, her blood vessels infused with alcohol.

"All the more reason to," Cassie laughed, sliding her Solo cup towards Jester and he dosed her a good one.

Britney nodded and Jester splashed some Jack into her cup. He leaned towards her, he gave her a soft smooch, causing her amber eyes to glow.

He gestured to Jes, and she fluttered her fingers. *Bring it on.* He laughed and poured. "Say when."

Jes shrugged *I don't know* and they both grinned. She soon placed her hand over the top but forgot to say stop and the whiskey dripped off her knuckles. Jester and Jes hee-hawed.

"Well, Jeez Jes," Cassie grumbled. "Just waste it."

"No wasting the booze. Only getting wasted allowed," Britney chuckled.

"Here, here," Jes said, lifting her cup to the sky and then taking a healthy gulp.

Jester smiled. He liked that about Jes, she could drink without pretending to be delicate or pretending she could handle her alcohol when she really couldn't. Jester tapped the bottle to Jes' cup in midair and then said, "Down the hatch," before taking a swig from the bottle himself.

"Yep. Bottoms up," Jes said, causing Britney and Cassie to go into stitches.

"Oh, you know what I mean," Jes said, and it sent the other girls cackling hysterically. "Now *here's* your bottoms up," she continued, turning her derriere from the back seat and twerked toward her friends which, of course, sent them into fresh convulsions.

"You like that, huh?" Jes said to her pals but then grinned at Jester, who mused inwardly: *Wow. That was actually pretty sexy*. He'd never thought about her in that way, but now he could see it.

Britney ceased laughing. She'd seen the flirting and now her lips were pulled tight.

"Babe," Jester placated. "We're just having some fun, right?"

"Lighten up," Cassie reprimanded Britney, and she immediately softened.

In those moments Jester could see how much Cassie influenced Britney. It just felt less like her caring for a friend and more like manipulation.

Jes made a face that only Jester noticed, and his lips tugged at the corners. With her face half hidden in the shadow of night, Jes' purple deformity was hardly visible. Too bad about that, he thought. She was a great girl, and she'd be quite pretty if it weren't for the port wine stain. She had that messed up arm, but it didn't inhibit her shooting abilities at the shooting range nor detract from her best features: her thick, shiny auburn hair and eyes, bright blue as the deep sea. He wondered if makeup would cover up that birthmark or if she could be a candidate for surgery, like Britney had undergone. *Britney*. Oh, right. Why was Jester thinking about *Jes* when he had his beautiful girlfriend right there beside him?

He must be drunker than he thought.

Except lately, *Jes* had been slipping into his thoughts more than Britney, and he couldn't ignore it.

CHAPTER TEN

"Hey, Astrid?" Jester called, waving at Astrid's mom as he bounded up the stairs, taking two at a time.

"Yo. In here," Astrid said, and Jester swung the bedroom door open. Astrid posed on the floor, reapplying polish to her toes in between her regularly scheduled pedi appointments.

"Nice," Jester said, gesturing toward Astrid's chosen polish color as he flopped onto her bed.

"Thanks. It's called Shiraz. Like wine."

The shade reminded Jester of Jes' birthmark. The reason he was here. "Hey, what do you know about using makeup to covering up deformities?"

Astrid glanced at him sideways, screwing the top back on the polish. "I know about covering up zits. Deformities? Not so much."

"Who does?"

"The internet. Dermatologists. Maybe some of the Blonde Squad girls. Depends on what kind of deformity. How severe it is. Who are we talking about?"

"Jes."

Astrid cackled meanly, checking if her toes were dry before collecting her mani kit and rising from the floor. "That's a lost cause."

"I don't think she is."

"Why do you care?" Astrid's lips quirked.

Jester rolled from his tummy to sitting position.

"Because she's Britney's best friend."

"And what else?"

"Maybe she just deserves a break in life."

"Like Britney got?" Astrid said.

"Exactly."

"Why not talk to Paloma and Tish? Ask them to give Jes a makeover, like they did for Brit." Astrid remembered the conversation with her fellow Elites and Squaders at Tish's house, discussing the idea of transforming another loser girl in the future.

"Why don't you?" Jester shot back.

"Because you're the one wanting it to happen! I couldn't care less."

"But you're the one with the little clique that makes things happen."

"For one thing, our clique is not 'little,' it's just exclusive. Being an Elite, school royalty, or Blonde Squaders, it's not gonna allow in everyone. Believe me, your Britney wouldn't even be on the middle step much less the tippy top rung if not for the metamorphosis."

"Okay, I get it."

"Do you, Jesse? Do you think for one minute you would have ever given Brit a second look had she not gotten that makeover?"

He wanted to protest, but deep down, he knew he was shallow enough that it was true. He *had been* physically attracted to Britney initially; otherwise, he might have taken a big no-go on her. He had viewed pre-Britney makeover photos, then with her eye and dental surgery. If he were honest with himself, Pre-Britney would never have become his girlfriend. But Jes...he had been drawn to her personality and their shared interests, despite her deformity. If Britney wasn't his girlfriend, would he have been captivated enough by Jes to still ask her out? Was he seeking Astrid's help now because he was curious to see if Jes could be beautiful enough that he would have gone for her without ever meeting Britney? Had he looked forward more to seeing Jes and planning their excursions together than he had for Britney? Jester's self-revelations startled him.

Astrid snapped her fingers under Jester's nose. "If you're gonna space off, I'll leave you to yourself."

"I wasn't spacing off. I was deep in thought."

"Yeah, I'll use that line in case I snooze in Mr. Hamlet's class this year. 'Sleeping? No sir, I was lost in introspection.'"

"You juniors have it so easy," Jester said. "Try that in twelfth-grade Social Sciences."

"Give me a break. Everyone knows the seniors rule the school. Even the twelfth-grade losers get special privileges. Hey, how about me giving you a pedicure?"

"I'll take a hard pass on that," Jester laughed.

"Come on. Be a sport. Let me paint your nails."

"No! Go torture someone else. One of your thousands of minions who sniff after you."

"Eeww. That doesn't sound right."

"You know what I mean. You got guys panting in the

hall, hanging on your last word."

"Who'd do about anything for me?"

"Yes, my beautiful Astrid. Star of the night."

"And day," she laughed. "Would *you* do anything for me?"

Jester groaned. "Here we go. I sense blackmail coming on."

"You're the one who wants me to liaise with Paloma and Tish. To help your other half."

Jesse's ears got hot, then realizing Astrid meant his and Jes' shared name.

"So, then you'll do it?"

"Of course, honey. And you're gonna do something for Astrid, right?"

"Can't you just do something for me without there ever being strings attached?"

"You mean because we have a connection?"

"Exactly." *Astrid's mom and Jester's dad.* "And if we didn't?"

"I wouldn't give you a second thought," Astrid smiled. It was a personal joke between them. Wouldn't give you a second thought, when you're number one in my mind.

"So, you'll talk to the Elites and Blonde Squad? See what they come up with?"

"So, you'll wear Shiraz on your toesies?"

Jester groaned. "You're trying to turn me into a metrosexual."

"Jesse, try to keep up. 'Metrosexual' is so nineties. It's 'Spornosexual' now. Here, stick those dogs up."

Jester kicked off his flip flops and bent his knees toward the ceiling. "Is this tickling your fancy?"

Astrid grinned, coating his big toe. "Oh, in such a big way."

"I'm sure this isn't the end of this. So what else am I gonna have to do to satisfy this deal with you?"

"Oh, I have some ideas. I'll let you know when the time comes."

"That's what I'm afraid of."

Astrid smiled. "Well, we're two minds of the same evil, right?"

He didn't answer, watching the beautiful girl giving him a glossy pedicure.

CHAPTER ELEVEN

"Okay, what's wrong?" Jester asked Britney, rolling out of bed and grabbing her clothes.

"I'm just not feeling this," she said, turning her back to him as she stepped into her underwear.

"Great. Perfect," Jester said, his woody turning to pulp.

"I'm sorry."

"I don't want you to be sorry. I want to know what the problem is." Jester glanced at his phone, which he had turned off when they had hopped in the sack. He noticed a couple of texts from his friends. Astrid's message said: "Tell your GF I'll expect her and Jes at the crib this evening."

"You made plans to meet Astrid?"

"What? No!"

"Okay. Well, you should probably double check." Jester pulled on his clothes; all hopes of doing the deed with Britney going down the drain.

"Who's asking you this?"

"Astrid."

"Why is she texting you?"

Britney's mouth puckered like she'd been sucking on Sour Patch Kids candy.

"What difference does it make?" Jester snapped, his pent-up sexual frustration affecting his tone.

Hurt, Britney blinked at him, and he regretted his response. "I didn't mean it like that. Astrid probably assumed you'd be with me or your besties. Guess she wanted you to get the message."

"Well…okay. But Paloma, Melody, and several of the Squaders and Elite's got my phone number, so why didn't she check with them? Why would she want to talk to me? We hang with some of the same people, but we're not exactly ride or dies."

"Dunno, why don't you text her and see?" He did know. That favor he'd asked Astrid to do.

Britney offered a nonchalant shrug as she flicked her hair over her shoulder. Jester's gaze traced her figure with an intensity that never failed to ignite his desire, but lately, an unspoken unease seemed to linger between them. Perhaps that unease was the reason she'd rejected his advances this afternoon. "So… what's wrong?" he prodded.

"You know," Britney answered.

"The same thing bothering you?" Ever since they had first started having sex, Britney had not only gotten more possessive, but she'd also gotten more paranoid. Britney had been a virgin, and it had taken months to get her to go all the way. She was reluctant to go to a doctor for birth control, afraid of her mom finding out. So, the responsibility of preventing little Britney's and Jester's running around, had fallen to Jester. On one occasion, the condom had broken. Another time, he'd forgotten to bring one and they had been in the throes of passion and had gone without. Oh, how good it felt to be without the thing pulling his skin and pubics. She hadn't been down for that again. Britney was afraid of getting pregnant. She said she loved Jester and enjoyed sleeping with him, but the burdens of worrying about getting knocked up had overwhelmed her. Jester had told her he'd marry her if that ever happened. But now that thought sent him into a panic. Britney was beautiful, nice, and loyal. All of Jester's buds were envious of him. Jester should feel lucky to have her, but lately...he felt out of sorts. And guilty. Because he knew why. And maybe Britney suspected too.

"Brit, baby girl, we'll be careful, okay?"

"No, Jesse, we haven't always been. And I can't take those chances." She slid on her sandals, the cue she wanted to leave before Jester's mom got home, not ever entirely comfortable in doing it at his house in case she came home from work early.

"Well, would you rather do...something else?" That meant hands or mouth instead of straight-on sex, someone giving and someone reciprocating. Britney wasn't a fan of giving but would if Jester asked super-nice for her to. After all, he'd done the same for her.

"I'm sure you'd be fine with something else," Britney said, her lips tight.

"I'm sure you would be too. You never had complaints about me doing that before."

"Just take me home already."

"Britney, what is *really* wrong?"

"We used to be alone together. Now we're always with Jes and Cassie."

"You're the one who invited them along. I thought

that's what you wanted. And we're alone right now!"

"I know. But I feel like you'd rather do stuff as a group now."

"You mean I'd like to have you, Cassie, and Jes in my bed?" He grinned at her sharp look.

"Oh, wouldn't that make you the most popular senior this year, your ménage a' trois plus one?"

"Def."

"I meant, we're hanging with Cassie and Jes all the time."

"What do you want from me? You wanted me to like your friends. So now I do."

"You tolerate Cassie. And pay too much attention to Jes." Britney crossed her arms over her chest.

Jester's ears felt warm. He reached over and turned on his ceiling fan. "Britney, you asked me to be nice to your friends, and I have been. Isn't that what you wanted?" Put it back on her. Blame-shifting.

"You're right. I'm sorry."

Jester relaxed, not feeling guilty because he had found himself thinking of Jes, instead of Britney, when they'd been in bed together.

"Jesse, are you thinking of breaking up with me?"

His shoulders cramped from tenseness. "What? Brit, that's what you thought? That's why you couldn't go through with doing it today?"

If she noticed he hadn't given her a 'No,' she didn't say it. "I just feel you're not into me as much as you were."

How did girls pick up on these things? Their vibes.

66

Of course, Jester wasn't about to tell her she was right. Anyway, who wanted to tick off the person they wanted sex from? Regardless of Britney's sixth sense, he'd deny it. He felt like a dog too, still wanting Britney to sleep with him - or all the other stuff, because she was the one available to him — even though Jester had his choice of several interested, single ladies. Not Jes.

Deflecting once more, he threw her a "Aren't you being silly" look. "I wasn't breaking up with you."

"Okay. Maybe I overreacted."

"Maybe you did. Maybe I should've been attentive to you."

"It's fine. I'm glad we're not breaking up."

"Me too." But Jester's inner voice whispered, "Are you really?" Ignoring the voice, he said, "So we're all still on for this weekend? Me, you, and the girls going to the Summer Bash fair?"

"Of course. They're hyped to go. We can't wait for the candy apples and funnel cakes."

"Ready to roll now?"

"If you want," Britney cocked her head toward the bed. "Instead. For a few minutes."

Jester's clothes were off before she'd even finished the sentence, and Britney giggled, kicking off her sandals and shucking her shorts and underwear. Jester tore the condom open with his teeth, slipping it on in record time, and slid inside her. "If we broke up, I'd miss this," Jester said, his mind filled with conflicting thoughts. He knew that breaking up would suck, especially right before school started back. Then again, he'd be free to…do whatever.

Britney said, "Me too," and continued to chatter a bit more about their situation.

Jester replied with a noncommittal, "Uh huh," not wanting further conversation as he focused on bringing Britney to climax first, then himself.

As they redressed for the second time, Britney kissed him and Jester said, "Don't forget to get back with Astrid or else I'll have her hassling me why I didn't give you the message."

But Jester couldn't help but think about Britney's words, about breaking up. As if they had spoken the words into existence, breakups loomed unseen in the air like stealthy aircraft.

CHAPTER TWELVE

"So, do you girls want soda, water, or something stronger?" Astrid asked Jes and Britney.

"You're joking, right?" Britney asked, tearing herself away from scoping out Astrid's house and noting the display of wealth. The high-quality furniture and clean, varnished walls were a far cry from her own home's self-assembly snap-together pieces (IKEA like bargains) and peeling, stained walls. Britney had figured Astrid came from bucks, but seeing it firsthand made her feel out of place, even if she'd been embedded into the Blonde Squad and Elites.

"About the booze? No, not kidding. My folks never keep it under lock and key. I can have some whenever I want," Astrid said, her tone casual.

"That's okay," Jes said, "water is fine. Your house is beautiful." She wanted to add how beautiful Astrid was, too, but thought it might be weird. Even weirder, this was the first time she'd ever seen Astrid without her fake eyelashes or her multiple layers of mascara.

"Bottled, iced or warm, or sparkling?" Astrid asked, roving around the kitchen and grabbing herself a ginger ale from the fridge.

Jes only had tap water at her house. Her single mother wouldn't waste money on bottled water when a cup run under the faucet would do. "Bottled. Cold, please."

"Brit?" Astrid asked, oblivious to Jes's sharp glance.

Only Jester and Britney's two best friends ever shortened her name. Jes mused, wondering if Britney was closer to Astrid than she let on.

"Perrier. With lime, if you've got some," Britney answered, shooting a look at Jes that said: I never said she could call me Brit.

"Got it." Astrid put the bottles of ginger ale, water, and Perrier in a carrying device with cup holders. "Follow me," she said, and the two girls trailed after her up the staircase.

Astrid's room was decorated with creams and smoke, accented with silver. Jes had only seen that kind of décor in magazines. Her own room was the same bubblegum pink she'd had since elementary school.

"How cool," Britney said, gently pushing a white swing hanging from the ceiling. A swing! In a bedroom!

"Go ahead," Astrid motioned.

"Naw, that's okay," Britney said, opting to settle beside Jes on a light grey settee with soft silver and white cushions.

Astrid sipped her ginger ale, then setting it aside as she opened drawers on a vanity table and placed mysterious boxes and tubes on the surface. "Jes?" She patted the high-backed seat.

Jes complied, not sure what Astrid wanted her for.

"Today is your makeover. Don't worry. I watched a girl on YouTube for tips. And this makeup is sterile, never been used before. Just bought them."

There were dozens of expensive-looking makeup brushes, applicators, and products.

"What? You bought me makeup?" Jes asked.

"Yeah. So, you can do it at home on your own, once you learn how," Astrid said, opening a jar.

"Wait. Jes, did you even want a makeover?" Britney asked.

"Didn't you?" Jes shot back, looking at Britney like she was nuts for asking. Was Britney jealous that an Elite was helping her, just like the Blonde Squad girls helped Britney?

"I know you can't afford treatments, so this is the next best thing. And some treatments can actually make it worse. I've been reading up on it," Astrid said, dipping a makeup brush in the jar.

"It?" Britney said.

"Port wine stains."

"You're gonna fix my birthmark?" Jes asked in amazement.

"Fix, no. Let's see how this works, and maybe a fix for you in the future. Cover up, yes." Astrid aimed the makeup brush at Jes's temple. "Can we clip your hair out of the way?"

Jes nodded, allowing Astrid to pin her glossy auburn hair back.

Britney believed it was a pivotal moment. Jes hated anyone touching or looking at her birthmark. She glowered at the others, but they didn't notice.

"When we're through, maybe do something with your hair? It's beautiful, your best feature. But it needs

71

to be trimmed up and styled to the shape of your face."

Jes's eyes glowed as she nodded at Astrid.

Britney remembered how Jes and Cassie had ragged on her about the Blonde Squad's makeover for her. All that animosity went right out the door as Jes readily agreed to Astrid's suggestion. Now Britney parroted back Cassie and Jes's snide remarks and conjecture about the Squaders at that time: "And you're doing this out of the kindness of your heart?"

"That, and your boyfriend asked me to," Astrid said, brushing primer over Jes's skin.

Britney shot up from the settee. "Jester?"

"That is your boyfriend, right?" Astrid's lips pulled at the corners.

"Of course. Why would he do that?"

"Because Jes is your best friend. And Jester wants you to be happy," Astrid said, squeezing something from a tube and applying it to Jes's cheek with a sponge.

It made sense. But Britney's stomach dipped for some reason. "But why would he ask you? Why not Paloma or Tish or another Squader or Elite?"

"Jesse's not a fan of any of them," Astrid said, smoothing the compound over Jes's cheek in a small circle. "He knows he can count on me for favors. That smile of his - who could turn him down, huh?" Astrid's own smile remained inscrutable.

"Astrid, do you like Jester or something?" Britney dared, holding her breath, risking upsetting their hostess and getting her and Jes booted out before Jes's makeover was complete.

Astrid's eyes zeroed in on Britney. "Yeah, I like him. Even love him."

Britney sucked in her breath, sinking back onto the settee. "Oh," was all she could manage.

Astrid threw her head back and laughed. "You do realize my relationship with Jester?"

Britney steeled her heart for what would come next. "How long?" she choked out. "How long have you been seeing him?"

"Oh, most of my life," Astrid smiled.

Oh wow, it was worse than Britney thought. How could she compete with a long-term connection? Even longer than her friendship with Cassie and Jesamean. "Then...you've been seeing him all that time?"

"Yes. He has stayed over here lots." Astrid seemed to be enjoying this, her lips pursing and her eyes sparkling. Jes was either too stunned by Astrid's revelation or too enamored with her transformation to notice Britney's distress. When Astrid noticed Britney's twitching mouth, she said: "But that's how it is when you have siblings."

"What?" Britney exhaled.

"I thought you knew. Jester's father. *Our* father. Different mothers. Different last names. Me, my father's; Jester's, his mom's." Astrid said, as she continued to apply creams and concoctions across Jes's skin.

"But...this isn't Jesse's house," Britney said, feeling ten pounds lighter after Astrid had explained her and Jester's relationship.

"No, he lives with his mom. Unless they can't get along, then he crashes here."

"I thought Jester could get along with anyone," Britney said.

"Yeah but dealing with parents is a lot different than with regular people," Astrid said, brushing some powdery stuff along Jes's jawline, then blending it over the rest of her cheek. "Well, are you ready for your result, Jes?" She swiveled Jes toward the vanity mirror.

Both Britney and Jes gasped. "What did you do?" Britney cried.

"I can't believe it," Jes sobbed, turning her head and looking at the side of her face from all angles.

"You like?" Astrid grinned.

"No, I love it," Jes continued crying.

"You're gonna cause your makeup to run," Britney said, giving Jes's shoulder an affectionate squeeze as she stood behind her.

"No, it's a concealer made especially for camouflaging birthmarks and scars. It's waterproof and smear-proof," Astrid explained. "But you gotta stop crying if you want me to do your eye makeup to pull it all together."

"Sure!" Jes exclaimed, and Astrid began applying shadows, liner, and mascara.

"It's amazing," Britney said.

"If you didn't know she had a birthmark there before, you'd never know it."

"Voilà," Astrid said, turning Jes so she could see her makeup.

Britney's mouth formed an O. Jes was actually beautiful!

"I can't believe it's me!" Jes cried.

Britney wondered if Jes would be invited into the Elites. She knew there was competition among the Elites and Blonde Squaders. Why would Astrid create more competition? Britney remembered how Paloma and Tish had taken credit for transforming her. Despite Astrid's claim that Jester had asked for his half-sister's help, would Astrid boast about having transformed a potential Elite?

"What do you say we hit a beauty salon now?" Astrid asked. "My treat. Got my own credit card from my parents."

"Just don't let the hair stylist dye Jes's hair," Britney said. "Her hair color is gorgeous as is."

"Wouldn't dream of it," Astrid said. "She doesn't need to be made into a blonde to fit in. No offense, Brit. Your hair looks great, the gold streaks make you mostly blonde, and it put you in with the Squaders. But Elites have no hair color requirements."

Britney let out a silent breath. So, then Jes would be recruited for the Elites.

"I could've gone lighter and gone Blonde Squad," Astrid continued. "But going darker actually made me more distinct."

"Wait. You're not a brunette?" Britney asked.

"No. Brownette. Not like the Urban Dictionary definition," Astrid added.

Jes nodded, even though she had no idea what Astrid was referring to.

"What's the deal with your lashes?" Britney dared.

"You mean double false lashes and lots of mascara? It's a way to stand out. Everyone knows Astrid for her dark hair and black lashes," Astrid said, smiling and beckoning the others toward the staircase.

"So, it's...a persona?" Britney asked as they waited for Astrid to unlock her BMW.

"Sure. But then we're all just putting on a persona, right?" Astrid asked, cranking up and zooming away with her passengers.

"With all respect," Britney said from the back seat, having lost when Jes called shotgun first. "But sorry, I think you look better without the lashes."

"Yeah? I look rockin' either way," Astrid grinned at Britney in the rearview mirror.

Both Britney and Jes laughed. "Yeah, you do," Britney agreed. "You sure do."

Britney mused about how Cassie would react to Jes's transformation and her newfound friendship with Astrid. She'd probably be so jealous.

CHAPTER THIRTEEN

Cassie adored Jes's makeover. But not receiving an invitation to Astrid's with Jes and Britney, or to the beauty salon where Jes had her hair trimmed, layered to give it volume, and highlighted to enhance the rich hues of mahogany, burgundy, and cherry, stung her.

"I'm sorry, Cass," Britney repeated for the tenth time as Cassie brought it up again, and Britney was now a little tired of it all. "Jes and I had no idea why Astrid summoned us. Besides, you don't even like Astrid."

"Neither did you," Cassie shot back. "You only tolerated her because Squaders and Elites hang out together."

"Right. But Astrid's not that terrible after all," Britney said.

"Was that before she splurged on you and Jes on your day trip and then a night on the town, or after you found out she's your boyfriend's half-sister?" Cassie folded her arms across her chest.

Okay, Cassie felt left out, and Britney justified her friend's snippy tone.

First, Britney had received eye and dental surgery, and now Jes had been given a new lease on life with her port wine stain cover up, a makeover, and a stylish haircut. Britney had become an auxiliary Blonde Squader, and Jes was in line for the Elites. Where does that leave me? Cassie thought. Unless…

"Listen, do y'all think you can put in a good word for

me with the Squaders and Elites? Maybe see if they want to hook me up with a makeover too?" Cassie asked.

Britney and Jes's exchanged glances, their beautifully made-up eyes shifting between Cassie and each other.

"Cass, Paloma, and Tish approached *me*, not the other way around. You know this, you were there. And Astrid asked about Jes," Britney reminded Cass.

"Well, looks like everyone's got someone to go to bat for them but me," Cassie said coolly.

"Look, Astrid helped me because her brother asked her to," Jes said. "Jester knows you don't really like him, so I'm sure his sister wouldn't be comfortable with us asking her to help you."

"Maybe I can understand that," Cassie said to Jes, "But what's your excuse, Brit?"

"Listen, do you really want Paloma or Tish or any of those Blondes or Elites to touch you after they've snubbed you and talked behind your back?"

"You know what's worse? Your own best friends snubbing you and talking trash about you," Cassie said in a wavy tone.

"We've never done that to you, Cassie!" Jes's voice pitched. "Should I have not taken Astrid's help? To not have found out that I can be pretty? You'd think you'd want me to be happy. Instead, you want me to be as miserable as you."

Cassie sucked in her breath, while Britney's eyes widened and Jes covered her mouth.

"I didn't mean it like it came out," Jes apologized.

"Well, looks like you girls got your butts in, Brit as a Squader and Jes a shoo-in for the Elites, even with your less than perfect arm," Cassie said, watching Jes cover her deformed arm with her other hand, shrinking into herself. "Can't expect them to lower their standards by accepting the pale and ugly fat girl too, huh?"

"Cassie, I'm sorry," Britney repeated again. "Maybe we can get Astrid to book you with her hair artist for a hair design or suggest a salon for a makeover for you. Please don't be mad at us!"

"Britney, listen to yourself. Hair *artist*?! A hair *design*? Normal people call it a 'hair stylist,' 'haircut.' You're starting to sound like those snotty girls you hang around with. And I'm not mad. I'm just miserable, right, Jes?" Cassie gathered her snacks and stuffed them in her backpack.

"Cassie, don't leave," Jes pleaded. "Stay. I'll use some of the makeup Astrid bought me and try to make you up the best I can, even though it's not my best skill." She began rummaging in her purse.

"Don't bother," Cassie said, tossing the backpack across her shoulders. "See? Apparently you gotta have a canvas to work off of. Britney had that body before Paloma and Tish ever took her under their wing to get her teeth and eyes fixed. Jes, you had beautiful eyes, hair, and skin before you ever got your birthmark covered up. I've got nothing. I'll just be the designated ugly fat friend, like *The Duff*. Just like

Bianca, I'm trying to reinvent myself instead of being the loser who hangs around with her two pretty popular besties. Epic fail, obviously."

"That's not true, Cass!" Jes said.

"Which part? Having the pretty friends, or me being fat and ugly?" Cassie asked, her hand on the doorknob.

"Don't do this," Britney said.

"Saying the truth?" Cassie asked.

"No, *lying* to yourself," Jes said.

"See, here's the thing, I'm the only one here *not* deceiving myself. Britney, I love you, but if you think Jester would have ever looked at you before the Squaders fixed you up, then you're crazy. And now with Jes's beauty shining, you better watch your boyfriend. The way he's been looking at her when we're all hanging out? He might decide to make a move now that she's gorgeous."

Jes's cheeks bloomed bright red. Britney's brows lifted up to her hairline.

"I'm sorry you're hurt, Cassie. I'm sorry if you feel we're passing you by. But I'm not sorry, nor is Jes, for accepting help to make our lives easier. And I'm sorry you can't be happy for us," Britney said.

"Oh, I can be happy for y'all. Doesn't mean I don't feel sad for what's happening to our friendship," Cassie said, closing the door and putting an end to any further conversation.

CHAPTER FOURTEEN

Just as Britney had caused a sensation the year before, Jesamean was Manatee High's IT girl this new school year, like she was influencer Hannah Bronfman. The crowded hallway split like Moses commanding the parting of the Red Sea, with Blond Squanders and Elites flanking Britney and Jes, and outcasts forced from the funnel as school royalty promenaded. Britney and Jes noted the stares of approval, whispers of "Wow, they slay," and "Yas kweens," and several wolf whistles as they passed by. Britney leaned in and said to Jes, "Don't worry, you'll get used to it."

Jes smiled, her slouch disappearing and her breasts held high. She noticed a star basketball player scouring her with his eyes. "I hope not," she said. "I want to remember this feeling forever."

School gossip buzzed about Jes's transformation. Some believed she had undergone surgery or laser treatment, while others attributed Jes's new look to the help of Paloma, Tish, or Astrid. Astrid, of course, got her glory, taking credit for Jes's metamorphosis.

Britney nodded, allowing Jes to bask in her moment. She had had her own after her eye and dental surgery. Britney surveyed the attention Jes was receiving from *lots* of guys and her stomach pitted with envy. While Britney knew her own looks turned heads, she now saw Jes exuding something she didn't have - an exotic allure with her thick, dark red hair, creamy complexion, and sapphire blue eyes. Jes had become a league of her own, no one in the Elites had glossy titian and cherry manes (unless they dyed it), whereas Britney was just another blonde. Just another one. Like all the Blonde Squad. This made Britney feel less special, similar to how Cassie might be feeling at this moment. Britney wasn't certain because she and Jes had barely spoken to Cassie since their falling out before the new school year began.

Last year, the three of them were inseparable, but things had changed. Cassie had distanced herself from them, unfollowing them on social media and refusing to respond to their calls or texts.

Cassie now sat alone during lunch. Yesterday, Britney and Jes held court with other Squanders and Elites while Cassie stuffed her face with Twinkies and Pringles. The duo had glanced over at Cassie, who pretended not to see them, preoccupying herself with unwrapping a Butterfinger.

Cassie's snippy words haunted Britney. She'd criticized Britney for relying on her surgeries to attract a guy like Jester, and while it hurt, Britney couldn't help but wonder if Cassie was right. Of course, Cassie had been wrong about Astrid; she wasn't a snot. Maybe a little stuck up at times to outliers, but she could also act friendly. Then again, that might've had to do with Jester, his telling his half-sister to sweeten up to Britney —and Jes.

As Britney navigated through the crowd of students by the lockers, she said to the Blonde Squaders and Elites, "Go ahead, y'all, I'll be along shortly," and she waited for Jes, who was engaged in conversation with two varsity football players in the middle of the hallway. Jes blushed at the boys' attention, unused to males fawning over her.

Britney nibbled at the corner of her mouth, remembering Jester's words to Jes the first time he had seen her after her transformation: "Wow, Jesamean, you're totally beautiful! I knew there was a bombshell under there!"

Jes had remarked: "Well, I was more hot mess than hot bae, but thanks!"

Britney felt the sting of jealousy at Jester's admiration of Jes. It brought to mind the recent incident when she, Jes, Jester, and Astrid were hanging out at Jester's mom's house. Britney catalogued how Jester's eyes followed Jes's every move, how they both laughed at the same things while watching Netflix's *Unbreakable Kimmy Schmidt*, and how they completed each other's sentences. Jester and Jes had numerous shared interests, like being fans of *Bizarre Foods: Delicious Destinations* and experimenting together with recipes from different cultures.

The way Jester had looked at Jes, the way they enjoyed each other's company, made Britney realize that she and Jester didn't have that same connection. When Jester drove Britney home later, she pointed out all those things, leading to a heated argument in the car. Jester had said, "You're overreacting and imagining things, Britney! Just chill already."

Then Britney said, "I could chill if you'd focus more on your girlfriend and less on my best friend."

Jester's eyes had flashed, crimson dotting his cheeks, the color like Jes's beautiful hair, then the redness spreading to his jaw and temples, much like Jes's birthmark. "You wanted me to like Cassie and Jes. Okay, so even though Cassie's not my favorite, I can tolerate her. And Jes turned out to be funny and sweet. But now you gotta problem with me being friends with her?" Britney's answer was to slam the car door behind her as she retreated.

Although Britney and Jester had reconciled the next day, their tension still lingered. Britney wondered if Jes could be the sole cause of their strain or was it something deeper. Shaking off her thoughts, Britney refocused on Jesamean. As she observed Jes attempting to make conversation with two varsity boys, struggling a bit, and awkwardly flirting with them, Britney couldn't help but notice that Jes never seemed to have any difficulty talking with Jester. Their conversations effortlessly flowed from topic to topic.

The two boys who had been chatting with Jes made their exit, and Jes waved at someone down the hall. The person enthusiastically reciprocated, their eyes filled with joy. They saw Britney beside the lockers, and the smile, once been reserved for her vanished.

Jester stepped forward and side-hugged Britney (like she was a freaking Duggar kid!), starkly contrasting their past affectionate gestures. Inside, Britney screamed at the realization. And his best smile? It flashed at Jes, not Britney.

Cassie's words echoed in Britney's mind once again. Yes, Houston, we have a problem.

CHAPTER FIFTEEN

Cassie folded her arms across her chest and asked, "What do you want from me? For me to say, 'I told you so'?"

"Instead of rubbing it in, why can't you say something to help me?" Britney asked.

"Help you? Like y'all helped me?"

Britney sighed. "Are you gonna repeat what happened last time we talked? I told you, Astrid didn't *ask* Jes if she wanted her help, she just *did* it. I'm not sure if either one of us would've accepted the Blonde Squaders or the Elites' help, had I known it would cause this rift between us."

"I'm happy for you, Britney. For real. But the great divide isn't between you and me. It's gonna be between you and Jes," Cassie said, offering a bowl of hot, buttered popcorn.

Britney's commitment to her diet plan paid off, evident also in Jes's transformation as she shed fifteen pounds, diligently following Britney's advice. However, the aroma of the snack proved irresistible, and Britney's willpower faltered. She scooped a handful of the tempting treat.

Cassie smiled, pleased her friend had indulged, like old times, and unconcerned about her own need to lose minimally one hundred pounds.

"No, the rift is between my boyfriend and me," Britney said, sipping a diet Coke while Cassie sucked down a large Arby's Jamocha Shake.

"Yeah, but the crap hasn't hit the fan yet with you and Jes," Cassie argued, her mouth full of popcorn.

"I'm not losing another friend," Britney said, daintily chewing popcorn compared to Cassie's wolfing.

"If you're talking about us, we can put this behind us."

"I want that. Why can't you do this with Jes?" Britney asked.

"Oh, I can. But you and she are going to go to blows, and I gotta pick sides now."

Britney snorted. "One, I'm not fussing with Jes. Two, no one has to choose sides."

"The fussing will come when your boyfriend fully goes after your gorgeous best friend. And I'll be forced to draw sides between you and her."

"Jes wouldn't do that to me," Britney argued, not sure if she truly believed it herself, catching a piece of popcorn on her tongue that Cassie had lobbed.

"But Boyfriend would."

"Then he wouldn't be my Boyfriend anymore."

"Exactly. You can kick Jester to the curb now and save yourself some heartache."

"I know you don't like him, Cass. But I don't want to break up with him."

"Make the first move. Don't be the one who gets broken up with."

"I don't want either of those things to happen," Britney said.

"Would you rather wait until he cozies up to Jes? Because whether you wanna turn a blind eye or not to the inevitable, or whether you believe Jes could betray you or not, something is gonna go down," Cassie said, polishing off the last of the popcorn, gesturing to the empty bowl, and Britney shaking her head, but Cassie popped some more anyway.

Britney would have defended Jes and Jester, had she been entirely certain that Cassie was mistaken. But now Britney didn't know which to believe—her heart, or Cassie's predictions.

CHAPTER SIXTEEN

The first blowup occurred during Homecoming week in October 2015. Though serious at the time, it proved minor compared to what came later.

Two weeks before the annual Homecoming game, students voted for the Homecoming Court. Last year, Tish, Paloma, Britney, and Astrid, along with two juniors and three senior girls, received nominations. All the nominees were either Blonde Squaders or Elites. As Manatee High's policy, two weeks before the annual Homecoming game, students took on the important role of voting for the Homecoming Court— a group of ten girls chosen to represent the school during the week's festivities. According to Manatee High's tradition, the final spot on the court wasn't chosen from the official list but left open for a *write-in candidate*—someone whose name students added to the ballot themselves.

Of course, some smart Alecs nominated Mickey Mouse, Harry Potter, and Scarlett Johansson. Melody ended up being the write-in. Britney gushed to her friends she was just happy to be nominated. However, this year, figuring maybe Paloma or Astrid would get Homecoming Queen, Britney hoped to secure the third spot, second place, or runner's up (called the Princess Triad). But then Britney almost swallowed her tongue when she learned that she hadn't made Homecoming Court, and had been selected for the coveted tenth spot, the write-in option instead.

Britney lost her breath when she saw Jes's name nominated for the Court. It stung even more because she'd been relegated to a write-in while Jes had jumped directly to Court. Last year, it had been unexpected and thrilling for Britney, but this year, it was unexpected and a letdown. Despite feeling like a loser, Britney knew she should be happy for Jes and grateful for the write-in spot.

At lunch, Britney glided toward the Blonde Squaders and Elites, plastering a smile on her face. Britney said to Jes, "Hey, congrats, baby. You did it!"

Jes squeezed Britney's wrist, her eyes damp. "Thank you! Can you believe I made Court? Pinch me, I'm dreaming!"

"Well, you deserve it," Britney said, her words ringing hollow to herself.

"Oh, Brit! Here I am going on and on. I'm sorry you didn't get nominated for Court."

"Not your fault," Britney said. Last year, Jes wouldn't have had a snowball chance in hell of getting this far. "I can still get the write-in," she added, wondering who else might be her competition.

"Oh, you will," Jes said, making false promises to cheer Britney up.

However, it didn't help. It reminded Britney of when she was skeleton-skinny, sight challenged, and her teeth all wonky. She felt like an outcast again, just as Cassie felt now. But Cassie had no idea how hard it was to be accepted into school royalty - the pressure to keep up, be in the right places with the right people, to be glammed up or to be "on" all the time, and have the right boyfriend, and to do things to keep him, sexual stuff. Before Britney become popular, she would have given anything to be the IT girl. But now, her limbs ached and she felt like she missed her full eight hours of sleep.

Still, Britney had won write-in, and there were appearances to keep up. Like when Britney and Jes accompanied Paloma, Tish, and Astrid to buy dresses for Homecoming. Britney and Jes headed for the sale racks, while the other three girls browsed in the designer section, the same place where Paloma and Tish had been picking out pageant gowns last year before entering high school.

Britney raised a brow at Jes. Even the discounted dresses were too expensive. Britney's phone pinged with a text. "Astrid wants us to come over there," she relayed to Jes, who groaned, "We can't afford anything over there! And if they're gonna show us their luxury threads, I'll be green with envy!" Despite their financial concerns, they skedaddled on over.

"So, this is how the other half lives," Britney whispered to Jes, petting a silk halter dress on sale, tagged $625.00. Jes's jaw dropped, saying, "We got no business in here. We can't even afford a scarf in this place."

Astrid sauntered over and said: "Okay, we have dressing rooms set up for us. I've already picked out a couple of dresses for you girls that are perfect for your coloring and bodies."

Jes gave Britney a look. But the dresses were not right for their pocketbooks.

Seeing their jumpy eyes cutting to each, Astrid said, "Don't worry about the price. Got it covered."

This was different from Astrid paying for Jes's makeup. It was a significant favor. Jes tried to refuse, but Astrid cut her off.

"It's on me. Daddy's credit card. Don't sweat it. He has no idea how many dresses I'm buying. If he gets a bill for three, so what? If he didn't want me to spend money, he wouldn't have given me carte blanche. Besides, Jester said I should do y'all a solid. He'd never forgive me if I didn't. And most importantly, you girls are Blonde Squaders and Elites. You gotta represent. You can't be embarrassing the rest of us by wearing cheap crap. Now, get back there and try on dresses. You're holding me up."

Britney and Jes practically skipped into the dressing rooms, Paloma twirled in a gorgeous red dress in front of three lighted mirrors. "You like?"

"Snatched," Astrid said.

"I can't choose. I might just buy them all," Paloma said, not at all concerned with the $700 price tag (or more) on each one.

Jes threw Britney a look. *See? They got money to burn. It's fine for Astrid to pay.* The girls scattered to their dressing room, the salesperson asking if they needed different sizes or help. They politely brushed her off and both of them exited their dressing rooms at the same time.

Britney, gilded in a dress with a slit up the thigh, glistened like a doubloon. Astrid was right, it was perfect for her smoking figure. The gold coloring brought out the amber of her eyes.

Jes modeled a midnight blue satin gown that molded to her body and made her sapphire eyes pop. The sheer sleeves camouflaged her disfigured arm.

Neither girl had ever looked so hot in their lives. And even though they were Blonde Squaders or Elites, the other girls sized up their competition. Astrid prowled in a white body-hugging gown that Jes wouldn't have had the nerve to wear.

"Isn't there a rule of etiquette about not wearing white after September?" Tish asked, decked in a purple one-of-a-kind dress.

"Not for Astrid," she shot it down, turning at different angles to view her ample bottom and cleavage.

"You gonna have to wear a good bra and panties for that," Paloma said. "Maybe get a skin toned body suit."

"Who said I was going to wear a bra and panties?" Astrid grinned.

"Every parent in the stands will have a heart attack," Tish said.

"You wear that? Next year the school will have a policy of having to pre-approve every outfit for the Homecoming Court," Paloma said.

But each was secretly thinking about how stunning Astrid looked in her outfit.

Jes and Britney tried on several dresses but decided on Astrid's selection for them. She had an eye for fashion.

Paloma purchased five dresses and Tish bought four. Astrid chose two and didn't bat an eye for the $5000 bill for hers, Britney's, and Jes's combined selections.

"Next, shoes," Tish said, heading over to an expensive footwear boutique in the mall. The girls chose two pairs each, Jimmy Choo kitten heels and Manolo Blahnik stilettoes. Of course, Jes and Britney's purchases were funded by Astrid.

"My brother will die when he sees you," she said to Britney.

"Well, we don't want that," Britney laughed. "Maybe just knock him out."

Jester had also made the Homecoming Court. As with the girls, only nine guys were selected, with one write-in. Tyne Dextander, the star basketball player at Manatee High, secured write-in. All Homecoming Court selectees would accompany each other on the football field, the girls and guys paired up in their nomination order. That meant Tyne would escort Britney at the big game's half-time ceremony. Then, once the announcer declared the winners, those chosen would stand abreast with their partner. That meant Homecoming Court, Princess/Prince Triad, then Homecoming Queen and King. Britney hoped she and Jester would win at least Triad so they might stand side by side together.

The night of the big game, the Homecoming Court mingled in the backdoor way of the concession stand, waiting for half-time. The crowd pumped with excitement, the Manatee's leading against the Coyotes by twenty-one points. An eighty-five-degree day had given over to a night in the low seventies, not too cold for some of the girls' strapless gowns – particularly Astrid's diaphanous white dress, and not too warm for the guys' suits and jackets. Someone had placed a sheet on the floor so the girls' dresses would not drag into spilled sodas and popcorn. There was chaos in the girls' bathroom, only one stall and one sink and mirror for them to check their makeup and hair. The guys made themselves scarce and let the girls pee and primp in the boys' room.

Everybody small-talked, not invested in heavy conversation. The girls were on live wires, wondering who'd get the vote for Queen. Paloma wanted it real bad, campaigning in the halls before the big day, saying to various girls, "Okay, chicks, remember a vote for me is a vote for you. If I win, I'm throwing a big bash at my house on Saturday and *everybody* is invited, even y'all who aren't in the Blonde Squad or Elites. This ain't no kickback party. Gonna have plenty of food. Might have booze. Might be skittling." The tease caused several girls to brighten, whispering amongst them and wide grins, even though they were outliers who Paloma would ignore for the rest of the school year. Paloma's spiel to the boys was almost identical, except she added: "Might be some tata's flashed. Some skinny dipping in my pool."

Even though Paloma was salivating to win Queen, she was a tenth grader, and sophomores rarely won. That spot usually went to seniors, although a few juniors had garnered the spot in past years.

Astrid had transformed into a mystical goddess, Aphrodite in a diaphanous white dress clinging to her voluptuous body, her long black hair hanging in ringlets. "Was there a fabric shortage in the market?" Jester asked, and Astrid giggled.

Although Jester had complimented Britney, he had barely had a conversation with her since. Britney peered at her empty hand, longing for Jester to lace his fingers with hers. They'd argued the night before – just another one of so many. The quarrel had been about Halloween coming up in a few weeks. In an effort to include Cassie, Britney wanted her, and Jes, to go to the Halloween Ghosts and Goblins Night with Britney and Jester. "I'm fine with Jes going with us, but I'm really done with Cassie," Jester had said. "It's not cool she's out there badmouthing me, especially since I've taken her along on most everything and if not for me, she'd been sitting her fat tush at home."

Britney had spat, "Well, I don't appreciate you talking about her like that," but Jester was adamant, insistent that Jes was in and Cassie was out. Britney hadn't told him that she was not wild about adding

Jes as their sole sidekick. It would have been fine if Cassie were going. But lately, with Jester and Jes joking around with each other, talking about their foodie food, being on the Trap Shooting Squad, and indie singers Britney wasn't familiar with (Angel Olsen's White Fire?), it made Britney feel like *she* was the third wheel.

Instead, Britney had said to Jester, "Just never mind. You don't have to take me or my friends. I'll just stay home," and Jester had shot back, "Great, I'll hang with my bros." And as much as Britney hated feeling like Jester liked her for the convenience of having someone around to have sex with, she offered to stay home with him and do what he wanted. At one time, he'd have jumped on it. But now, every squabble widened the abyss, making her think that they'd bust open the next big fight. Then who'd he turn to? Jester had girls panting for him, had dated or slept with many of the Blonde Squaders and Elites.

Britney glanced at Jes, reapplying her lipstick, a bold, ruby that would have looked clownish on Britney. Jes's eyes sparkled like a deep blue lagoon. Her shiny auburn hair, tipped with raspberry, reminded Britney of an Ever After High Mira Shards doll. Britney wondered, if Jester turned to Jes, would she make him her man?

Her musing was interrupted when Paloma squealed, "The football players are off the field. We're up next!"

The Court lined up, with nominees partnered up for

Triad, Queen, and King, and lastly write-ins. Britney linked arms with Tyne.

As Jes passed the cheering football crowd in the stands, she espied Cassie, munching a hot dog. Cassie did not wave. She clustered with some kids Jes wasn't acquainted with but recognized them as outcasts. Just like she and Britney used to be. Jes's stomach clenched. Jes was shuffling in front of Britney, so she couldn't see her reaction to Cassie.

Why couldn't Cassie at least acknowledge her? Britney thought. Just stuffing her face again and ignoring her. Britney knew it was unkind, but Jester was right, Cassie had put on way too much weight! Britney had offered to help the obese Cassie with her diet, with working out. But she'd refused. Britney knew Cassie's battles, but it was no excuse for her not to even try.

Cassie stared at her beautiful friends. Britney had reached out to Cassie to put theirs and Jes's friendship back together again. Cassie had thought it was what she wanted too. But it had been hard enough to be around the beautiful and popular Britney. Now there was Jes! She couldn't say that to them very well, could she? She thought she could be gracious and supportive, and she had tried. But it was too hard. And Cassie couldn't do it anymore. Just a blow to her spirit. Just another one.

The Court dropped the arms of their escorts, standing side by side on the artificial turf, half of the group angled to the right and the other half to the left. The center space on the field was reserved for the King and Queen. The announcer's voice rang out over the stands, "Manatee High's Homecoming Court for 2015 includes..." He read off their names and grades.

"Third runner up, Britney Glascier and Jorge Ortega!" Britney squealed and the couple strode up to the principal, who placed a bouquet in Britney's arms. She and Jorge waved to the crowd, taking their designated space as the first of the Triad.

Britney gazed at Jes, who gave her a thumbs up. She cut her eyes to her boyfriend, who smiled back. He waited with the only girl out there that Britney could trust him with — Astrid, who more than likely would come up to the Triad next.

"Second runner up, Astrid Grooms and Chaney Smith!"

The stands rumbled in response to Astrid's transparent white gown. Football players on the sidelines paused, helmets in hand, their gazes fixed on Astrid's fluid-draped body, like a cello waiting to be played. Britney imagined Astrid would be the talk of the school on Monday. She squinted toward the bleachers. Astrid's daddy pretended not to notice his daughter's see-through dress. Her mom smiled proudly, unconcerned with Astrid's gown selection. She knew Astrid sported nude-colored panties and a push-up bra underneath. Anyway, Astrid was classy, not a trashy thot. Jester's mom sat close by, unintimidated by her ex-husband's second wife.

Britney remembered Jester saying that any tension between them or her ex had long been dissipated. There had been some bitterness right after they had split up, Jester's mom going to court to change Jester's last name to her maiden name. Even after Jester's mom and dad had made nice, the name remained. It was why Jester's surname was Pynes and his siblings' last name was Grooms. It was why Britney hadn't realized at first that Astrid was Jester's younger half-sister.

Paloma breathed in deeply, all her teeth exposed in her anticipation. Of course she would be Homecoming Queen, she mused. She'd campaigned hard. Paloma's celebratory party on Saturday would be lit. Even though she'd promised every student they'd be invited, she'd enlist one of the wrestling team guys to stand guard at the door. Explain to those basic rejects that Paloma's parents had capped the number of people she could have over. Like they'd challenge someone built like Roman Reigns. If the outcasts thought they'd YOLO at her crib like they were snowflakes, they'd find out differently.

"First runner up, Paloma Brigh and Devon Amstead!"

Paloma's face contorted. If not for Devon grabbing her arm, she might have stayed rooted in shock. He nudged her toward the principal, congratulating them and presenting Paloma with a bouquet. She corrected her expression, smiling like everything was great- after all, she was a pageant girl and knew how to play the game. She and her Prince moved into the Triad, completing it.

Paloma didn't win Homecoming Queen! Britney mused. Then who did?

A mumbling flittered through the stands, the crowd voicing their curiosity as well.

Jes wondered if it was one of the seniors. Or even Tish?

"Ladies and Gentlemen, the 2015 Homecoming Queen and King for Manatee High School are: Jesamean Marcos and Jester Pynes."

The Elite and Blonde Squader girls' mouths formed an oval.

Jes's ruby lips parted wide. Jester dragged her out of her shock, arm in arm toward the principal. He congratulated them and placed the crown on Jester's head and then awkwardly attempted to place Jes's on her noggin. It knocked askew and Astrid handed off her flowers to her Prince and stepped up, securing Jes's tiara with a couple of her own bobby pins. She took the bouquet from Jes's hands to free her up, knowing what was coming next and wondering how onlookers would receive it.

Britney stared at Jes, who looked every bit like the royalty she had become, reminiscent of the beautiful redheaded queen in the painting The Accolade, except with darker crimson hair. Jes had been named the winner! And Jester. How did this happen? Shouldn't Britney be queen to Jester's king?

Amidst the roaring crowd, Britney refocused as the

announcer's voice pealed. What was happening?

"And now for a Manatee High tradition, as every Homecoming Queen and King has done since the school's inception in 1965, it is time for the royal kiss between the Court's number one couple," the voice echoed, and feet pounded against the bleachers, the crowd shouting "Go! Go! Go!" as if rooting for their football players charging down the field.

Britney's pulse ticked up, the crowd crying "Kiss, kiss, kiss!" Britney knew everyone expected a kiss between the Homecoming Queen and King. But she had thought it would be she and Jester. Okay, she could handle this. Just another time-honored deal. Just another one. Her boyfriend and best friend would share a simple peck.

But as Jester leaned in, it seemed personal. At least that's the way Britney interpreted it. Jester and Jes faced each other, and he drew her in gently, his fingers wrapped around her lats, and her fingers laced behind his nape. Their bodies pressed together, nary a space between them. Britney's ears buzzed like she'd walked under a live wire, the crowd's cry ratcheting up as the couple's kiss deepened. Britney grasped her Prince's forearm lest she'd faint. Jes and Jester's closed their eyes, their faces blending, and Jes's glossy curtain of hair shadowing Jester's face. This was no tiny, friendly peck; it was full on suck face.

Exhaling the breath she had been holding; Britney waited for the couple to come up for air. But they didn't.

Their foreheads remained glued together, their crowns snagging on each other like embattled kudus. But this was no blood match. This was giving in to what they wanted. Britney swore she could hear Brandon Flowers singing "Can't Deny My Love."

The crowd laughed at the entanglement, while Jes and Jester reaching up simultaneously to unhook their crowns. Their hands brushed against each other, something oddly intimate, and then outright intimate when Jester took both crowns and tossed them aside. Britney fumed, wondering what would happen next – would Jester start undressing them?

The crowd's excitement grew with shouts and cheers jabbing the air. Britney zeroed in on Cassie, who'd abandoned her chow down to study the Jester/Jes show. The announcer provided a play - by - play like a sports commentator, while the principal frowned and twitched, glancing toward the discarded crowns and then the couple exploring each other's mouth. The school had never witnessed a King and Queen engage in such a prolonged kiss. The principal scratched his head at this upend in tradition, two seconds from putting a stop to their passionate display.

Jester not only tongue-massaged Jes's gums but also planted kisses along her neck. The crowd erupted in, "Oooohh!" Britney refused to let them see her fall apart, but tears stung the back of her eyes. Jester ceased trailblazing Jes's throat, returning to her mouth, his hunger evident. For Britney, it felt like an eternity, torturing her, although it was likely only a matter of seconds.

Finally, the principal had enough of the PDA. He firmly placed a paw on Jester's shoulder, and Jester and Jes reluctantly disengaged. One of the Court's Princes picked up the crowns from the ground and handed them to Jes and Jester. Jester placed the tiara on his Queen's head, and she reciprocated crowning her King. The announcer's voice echoed across the field: "Ladies and Gentlemen, well, as much as we hate to interrupt young love, we do have a football game to get back to." Laughter erupted over the stands.

Young love? Britney's face crumbled. Was that what this was? She shot a glance at her best friend and boyfriend. *How could you even?* But they were staring into each other's eyes and didn't immediately notice her. Jes's head dipped, as Jester noticed Britney's eyes like amber ice cubes. Jester didn't seem guilty or sorry, instead, he averted his gaze and grabbed Jes's hand.

"Ladies and Gentlemen, this concludes our half-time event. Manatee High School Homecoming Court for 2015, please exit the field," the announcer said.

Jester and Jes grinned, waving at the crowd, whose applause thundered. The King and Queen took a few steps forward, but then Jester halted, prompting Jes to raise her brows. She giggled in glee as he scooped her up effortlessly, like a football player cradling the ball, carrying her across the field as if she were weightless, resembling a bride being hoisted over the threshold, as Jes's shiny auburn hair cascaded over Jester's shoulders.

The Court trailed behind them, and Britney bit her lip to hold back her tears.

On Monday, the gossip wouldn't zizz solely around Astrid's translucent gown; it would also include how Britney got royally dissed by her best friend and boyfriend.

CHAPTER SEVENTEEN

Britney stormed from the football field into the parking lot, and as she realized she had ridden with Jester, she said from between clenched teeth, "Oh, freaking great." She grabbed the hem of her gown and maneuvered through bumper-to-bumper vehicles, regretting her choice of three-inch heels instead of the kitten heels.

Britney's heart sank as she reached for her phone to call her mom, but the realization hit her hard. Her mom had missed the Homecoming due to work, and everyone Britney knew was back at the field. She chewed at the corner of her mouth, the anxiety vibrating through her.

A blur zoomed by and screeched to a halt. Cassie, in her mom's car, called out the driver's side window, "Your chariot awaits."

Britney hesitated but then climbed in. Where else was she going to go?

"What are you going to do?" Cassie asked, gripping the steering wheel as they merged onto the highway. "Forgive them? Cuss 'em out? Nothing?"

Britney's phone buzzed incessantly, flooding her with texts and missed calls from Jes and Jester. With each notification, she tightened her mouth. "Forgive them? No. Cuss 'em? Maybe. Do nothing? No, it'll be something."

"Like...?"

Britney ignored Cassie's inquiry, her mind racing with a thousand potential conversations she could have with Jes and Jester. Leaning her head back and closing her eyes, she tried to process her emotions.

Once Cassie dropped her off, Britney placed her bouquet in the fridge to keep it fresh, then hung up her beautiful gown. Removing her Astrid-like fake lashes, she cleansed her face of makeup, wishing she could wipe away just as easily the ruined evening caused by Jes and Jester.

Her phone buzzed again. Speaking of, she thought. Britney slowed her breathing, feeling the boiling inside of her chest robbing her of oxygen. It was now or never. 'What do ya got to say for yourself, prick?"

"Okay, Brit, can we have a chilled conversation? Or are you going to resort to name calling?" Jester said.

"Oh, I haven't even got started on the name-calling, Jesse."

"Britney, I wanna explain what happened tonight."

"Explain? It was obvious. You and Jes, thirsty."

"It was a joke."

"You're right. A real joke, Jester. Like your true name."

"No, I mean it was a prank, Brit. Me and Jes, we were punking you."

"Oh, that's what you're calling it now? Gee, where were the hidden cameras? Ashton Kutcher jumping out?"

"We thought you'd get it," Jester said.

"So y'all were trying to get one over on me?"

"Exactly."

"Well, you got it. Goals."

"I told him it went too far," the female voice said.

"Jes is with you!?" Britney cried. "I'm hanging up!" It was too much. Jester spews nonsense while his new significant other listens in.

"Don't!" they both shouted simultaneously, obviously on speakerphone.

"Britney, just listen," Jes said. "Jester and I didn't expect to win Homecoming Queen and King. We both thought it would be Paloma. We hoped it would be you and Jester."

"So, I suggested to Jes we should shake things up," Jester picked up the conversation. "This is my last year. Let Manatee High know this is how their seniors roll. Principal Wordell has a stick so far up his brown eye. Figured he wouldn't know what to do if his students went beyond a four-second kiss. Couldn't very well make a stink on the field or give us demerits, could he? So, fifteen seconds before we took our place at center field, I ran it past Jes. We thought you'd get it."

It was the lamest thing Britney had ever heard. "Yeah, I got it. You and Jes had to cook something up to cover what really happened. Jes is the swan. I'm last year's flavor. Y'all been fighting it for a while. Well, nothing to hold you back now. I'm letting you go, Jester. And you too, Jes."

"Come on, Brit! You're making this a big deal, and it's not!"

"Oh, it's a very big deal, Jesamean. To lose a boyfriend and best friend, all in one day."

"You don't have to lose anybody, Britney," Jester said, exasperated.

"Unfortunately, I do. Good luck. Wedding bells and babies in your future," Britney said, relieved they weren't on Facetime, as tears crawled down her cheeks. "Better be going."

"No, Britney," they both said at the same time but met with dead air.

Britney finally let the sobs come, knowing this was just the beginning of her pain.

CHAPTER EIGHTEEN

Jesamean and Jester didn't just humiliate Britney — they also lied about it! Britney had to skip Paloma's party because those two jerks would be there. The aftermath of Homecoming played out like a never-ending digital drama across Instagram, Snapchat, Facebook, and YouTube. In a series of uploads, Jes and Jester were captured in moments that teetered on the edge of impropriety, leaving viewers almost urging them to "get a room." Yet, the most agonizing chapter unfolded within the school's hallways. Laughter echoed down corridors, and conversations lingered by lockers, an orchestra of mockery conducted by the entire student body. Even Britney's loyal circle of Blonde Squaders and Elites couldn't resist the allure of the gossip, surrendering to the current of shared whispers and online rumor-spreading. When Britney spotted Jes and Jester laughing together at lunch at the benches, she pivoted and rocketed away.

Cassie steered Britney past the gossiping cliques, gripping her elbow. "What happened with dickhead and Jes? Spill tea now."

"What's there to tell? I called out Jes and Jester over the phone. They were together Friday night after Homecoming. No surprise there. It made the breakup easier and harder at the same time. I only had to have one conversation instead of repeating myself. They tried to convince me it was all a misunderstanding on my part. That they punked me."

"Like *Impractical Jokers*?"

"Yeah, but it felt more like *Scare Tactics*," Britney said, ignoring the cackles and pointing by the lockers as she spun her lock. "Awesome. I just broke a nail."

Cassie inspected it. "Got Super Glue? Wait a minute. This was supposed to be a senior prank? I don't get it." Every year since the school's inception in the 'sixties, the seniors plotted the most outrageous stunts. They'd stick Kotex's on all the windows in B-Wing, hoist granny panties up the flagpole alongside the Stars and Stripes or unleash crickets in the lunchroom. Fun and games unless they got caught. Those who got busted earned demerits, afterschool punishments like helping the janitor clean the student bathrooms, or even suspension, depending on the severity and impact of the prank.

"Yeah, I'm pretty sure the prank ploy was just an afterthought for Jesamean and Jester once they realized that the whole world saw them playing tongue tickle to the tonsils," Britney said, chucking books in her locker and lightening her book bag.

"Did they really think you'd buy that?" Cassie asked, cutting her eyes toward a blast of snickering. This time the laughter wasn't aimed at Britney, but at Cassie, who had to squeeze through the narrow hallway with her 250-pound-plus body.

"Obviously. If they just don't care how I feel, fine. But

to act like it was all in good fun? Like they're actually not into each other when we all know it's a lie, is just inexcusable."

"And douchey," Cassie added.

"Def. So, I just can't. But it's gonna make it hard. We're all in the same cliques. Can't avoid them."

"You can always come back to where you started from," Cassie said, joking but not joking, referring to when Britney, she, and Jes had been besties in their own group.

Britney mused, shivering inwardly, thinking of their loser group. "No," she said, locking eyes with Cassie. "Somebody said it in a quote. Something like, 'Minds that are stretched by new experiences can never go back to old dimensions.'"

"Yeah, guess you're right," Cassie said, frost creeping into her tone. "The Snakes said it better, 'Can't go back.'"

"The Snakes?"

"A band in the nineties."

Britney had forgotten that Cassie loved classic rock and metal. "Right."

"Just know, Brit, you walk away from me, you might not have anybody left," Cassie said, as the bell alerted students that they had three minutes to get to their afternoon classes.

"I'm sorry, Cassie. We'll always be friends, but it won't be like before."

"Yeah, sorry but not sorry, huh?"

Cassie stepped back, allowing students into the

the classroom before her, enduring their snorts as she crammed herself through the narrow doorway. She stiffened when Britney touched her shoulder. "Don't," Cassie said.

Britney's hand dropped. "Cass, we can still hang sometimes."

"No, we can't. You don't really want to, and I don't either. You'll move on from Jester. Will probably have a new boyfriend in no time. And who needs Jes, right? We've all moved on. I already have. Got a new misfit group. Fatties, pimple-faces, and weirdos."

Seconds before they'd both be late to class, Cassie heading to tenth grade Science and Britney to her elective class down the hall, Cassie said, "You know, you're no different than Paloma or Tish or Astrid. I know you think you are, and you'd think you would be, coming from the lowest rung group on campus to sit in the catbird seat. But you're just as much a snotty snob as them. Worse. Because you should know better. So, cry me a river that you got played by your boyfriend and best friend. We all saw it coming. Only *you* have been blind. And ungrateful. You made third in the Triad! You've had an amazing life for over a year, with a hot boyfriend. So go boo-hoo your crocodile tears, Britney. No one, including me, feels sorry for you. You wanna feel sorry for someone? Let it be for every loser kid here who wonders what it's like to be the IN one, who wonders what it would be like to not get made fun of or bullied every day of their life. Do you remember, Britney? Or along with becoming immune, are you brain dead to the memories?"

Cassie disappeared, and the bell rang. Britney trudged instead of rushing to her class, sore from her reaming.

CHAPTER NINETEEN

So, Jes and Astrid were besties now. That's what everyone was saying at school. It made sense, Britney mused, since Astrid had taken Jes under her wing and turned her into her pet project. Rumors circulated that Jes underwent laser treatment for her port wine stain, and it seemed to work. Astrid being Jes's boyfriend's half-sister just made the connection even stronger. On the other hand, Britney still hung with the Blonde Squad and Elites, her usual companions. However, her posture stiffened whenever she was around Jes, and she fidgeted nervously, struggling to maintain eye contact. Britney's new thing was to make a quick exit and be by her lonesome. She had no boyfriend since breaking up with Jester, but many guys trailed her. Britney buckled down on her studies, as there was nothing else left to do. At least she could get a leg up with qualifying for college in two years. Britney also watched a lot of old movies, reminiscing about the times when she, Cassie, and Jes would gather at each other's houses, snacking and commenting on movies like *Picture This* or *She's All That*.

Britney knew she should get a new boo right away and rub it in Jes's and Jester's face, but her sadness and anger had sapped her energy. Besides, dating any popular guy would mean running into Jester and Jes at their hangouts.

Britney removed all the pictures of Jester and herself from her bedroom. She also stripped her room of any remnants of Jes and Cassie. Additionally, she deleted her profile photos from Insta and Facebook, the ones where she and Jester were smiling and holding hands.

Several weeks had passed since Homecoming. Britney heard that almost every Blonde Squader and Elite planned to attend the upcoming Halloween bash. Jes and Jester had posted pictures of their costumes on social media, with Jester going as the Joker and Jes as Harley Quinn. Britney eyed their pix and decided not to go to the party. However, while browsing Pinterest, she stumbled upon a Poison Ivy costume that caught her eye. She knew she would rock that outfit with its bright emerald bikini, garter wraps-tights, and thigh-high shiny boots. The long red wig included, clenched it for her. Jes wouldn't be the only beautiful redhead in the room, and it didn't matter if Jes and Jester were dazzled; all that mattered was that Britney knew *she* was hot stuff. If this costume didn't grab the attention of every guy there, nothing would.

And she was right. The Halloween Ghosts and Goblins bash was in full swing, and *everyone* told Britney she looked dope. Paloma donned a ginormous silver ball gown reminiscent of TV's *Gypsy Sisters*, complete with a glistening crown and train. She nearly knocked over several Elites when she spun around. Britney couldn't even hazard a guess how much the thing cost. Tish channeled Elvira: Mistress of the Dark, her long black fall competing with Astrid's usual long black mane, except today, Astrid's dark locks were hidden under a blonde floor-length wig. Astrid's Lady Godiva costume, consisting of nothing more than a bodysuit, caught everyone's eye. Everyone momentarily forgot about Britney's outfit amid all the attention on Astrid.

As Jester and Jes strolled in, Britney heard them laughing then freezing upon seeing her. "Hello, former bestie and ex-BF," she sing-songed despite her heart lurching at the sight of them with their fingers entwined and in-love eyes for only each other. "Got any pranks cooked up for the night? Or do we only do Homecoming?"

Jes cut Jester a look, and Jester ignored Britney's shade, saying, "You look beautiful, Brit."

Jes eyed them both, finally relenting, "You really do, Britney. That body. You could wear a sack and still look good."

Since Jes was being gracious, Britney said, "Thanky, thanky. And if you remember, I did wear sacks – and you, until the Blonde Squaders and Elites took us from normcore to bougie."

Then Jester had to ruin the moment. He stared at Jes, not Britney, and said, "Well, y'all sure got flex now." An electrifying surge swept across the room, capturing the attention of the three friends and directing their gazes towards the origin of the elan.

Astrid's promenade through the room set every

male's tongue to panting.

"Working the room, I see," Jes said, smiling as Astrid waved at them. The three of them burst into laughter when a guy staring at Astrid boomed into a wall.

It felt like old times when the three of them – four with Cassie, hung out together. But it wasn't like old times. Jester had fallen hard for Jes, and Jes had betrayed their friendship. "You kids enjoy yourself," Britney said, eager to distance herself. "I gotta quota up before Astrid steals all the studs."

As if he read her mind, Baron Dise said, "Hey Britney, wanna go make out in the Haunted Room?"

She plastered her 100-watt smile. "Why not? Then you'll buy a girl a drink?"

"For certain," he grinned, sliding a hand against the small of Britney's back, guiding her toward the line of people waiting to enter.

The room was dark as a coffin, several screams ringing out as Goblins and Beasts jumped out at the high schoolers. Tish screeched as she plowed into a giant spider web, causing a couple of Blonde Squaders to giggle. Several low intensity bulbs came on, bathing everyone in yellowish lights. Seeking more darkness, Baron pulled Britney into a small space between Ghost Guy's hiding place and Satan's Lair. Baron laid a kiss on her, nice at first, then getting too extra with his squiggling tongue. When Baron's hands began to wander, she grabbed his wrist, saying, "Ain't on the menu." Baron had gone deaf, slipping a finger inside Britney's top and tweaking her nipple. If Britney screamed, no one would pay her any heed, screeching girls ran amok as creatures and demons chased them. She stomped his metatarsals with her three-inch boots, causing him to retract his hand. She then pivoted and almost ran smack into Jes and Jester.

"Y'all having a good time?" Jester asked.

"We were. Baron now? Not so much," Britney said.

"Where did you leave him?" Jes asked.

"Bloodied and damaged in the corner." Britney demonstrated a little kick.

"Oh yeah?" Jester said, tilting his head and looking around the wall.

"Blimp alert," Melody called, while Paloma knocked over people with her oversize gown, resembling a bowling ball smacking down pins.

Jes thought Melody was referring to the dress, then said, "Cassie at five o'clock." Jester's brows pulled tight.

What is she doing here? Britney thought. The Ghosts and Goblins Haunted House was only for Elites, Blonde Squaders, and school royalty. Tish's dad had paid for the event, assuring that outliers would not be allowed in.

Cassie was garbed as Princess Leia, with twin buns on the sides of her skull and a white dress. Britney suspected that Cassie's costume was made from a bedsheet since Cassie's mom couldn't afford a store-bought outfit for one-time use. Backlit by the sickly, yellow light, Cassie seemed to be bra-less or without undies, a look Astrid could carry off but not Cassie.

"What are you doing here, Cass?" Britney asked.

"Same as you, Brit. Living large."

A school royalty eleventh grader said, "You be that, babe. Super living large," as Britney and Cassie ignored her.

"You shouldn't be here, Cassie," Britney whispered.

"Oh, I'm sorry. Is this only for the special people?"

"I meant, you're just gonna get remarks like you just did. I just don't want to see you get your feelings hurt, Cass."

"Don't worry, Britney, I'm not gonna. I'm thrilled to be invited."

"Someone *invited* you? Who?"

"The Blonde Squad. Specifically, Paloma and Tish."

Both Britney and Jes gaped at the mention of the girls, who were standing a distance away. But why?

Cassie explained, "I think they're gonna transform me like they did for Britney, and Astrid did for you, Jes. Just think, I'll be a school royal, too."

Britney's heart sank. That couldn't be true. What was going on? Nothing of the sort had been spoken to her.

Jes couldn't believe it. She and Britney had been blank slates to work from. But Cassie…Jes didn't want to be unkind, but Cassie did not fit the mold. And while there were curvier girls, Kardashian type girls in the Elites and Blonde Squad, no fat girls would ever be allowed in. Especially not homely fat girls. What could Tish and Paloma possibly be thinking?

Jes stepped toward Paloma and Tish, and Jester busied himself elsewhere. "What are you doing?" she spouted.

"Doing? Same as you," Paloma said, scrunching up her gown to get it out of the way.

"You know what I mean."

"Oh, about Cassie? Aren't you happy we're including your little friend?" Tish asked.

There was a small silence.

Jes stared at her. Cassie was certainly not little. And she wasn't even sure Cassie was her friend anymore. "So, this is y'all's way of letting her in as your next remodeling project?"

The duo glanced at each other, then at Jes. "You could call it that."

"I call it bullcrap," Britney said, coming up behind Jes and towering. She was five feet ten in stocking feet and a giantess in her three-inch butt-kickers. "What's the *real* reason you called her here?"

"We can do for Cassie what we did for you," Paloma explained. "And Jes," she added, Astrid joining them. "But Cassie will need a smidgeon more help, right? So, if she wants it, she'll have to fight for it."

"What does that mean 'fight for it?'?" Britney asked.

"You can't be a Blonde Squader if you're not blonde. You're not gonna make the cut into Elites unless you're Elite, moneyed, or extra. And you don't get to be school royalty if you're not beautiful, unique, or bring assets. Cassie's got none. So, she's got to do what we ask if she wants in," Paloma said.

"She'll have to lose a ton of weight, that's a given," Tish added. "Will have to dye and style her hair, get good clothes, and get an exceptional make over, which is where we come in. You're with us, right, Astrid?"

The space between Astrid's perfectly tweezed eyebrows crinkled. It was first time she was hearing about Cassie getting subsumed into the Elites. "Fine," she relented.

"Jes? Britney?" Tish asked. "All the girls are in on this already."

So, everyone knew but Britney, Jes, and Astrid, Jes mused to herself. "This seems sketch. What's in it for y'all?"

"Entertainment," Tish answered, her lips pulled into a smirky smile.

"She's not y'all's entertainment," Britney snapped. "She's a human, with feelings."

"She's the biggest loser in the school!" Paloma cried. "She's gonna get a chance she'll never get again!"

"And what's that gonna cost her?" Britney asked.

"How much did it cost *you*, Britney?" was Paloma's salty snap back.

It dawned on Britney that Paloma hadn't answered the question. "If you're gonna give her a makeover, what's she doing here now?"

"Look at her!" Tish cried. "She's wearing a freaking sheet like it's a toga party! She needs help ASAP."

"And you're going to do something for her here at

a Halloween party?" Britney asked.

"No time like now time, right?" Paloma smiled. "But first, Cassie's got to pass a teeny test."

Before Jes could ask what that was, Tish called, "Cassie, you ready?'

Cassie waddled over, like Paloma's waddling all evening in her humongous gown, except Cassie's waddle wasn't due to a costume, rather her sausage rolls. Britney thought she came over like a summoned puppy.

"What test, Paloma?" Britney persisted.

"Like an initiation," Cassie answered.

Britney and Jes shared a mutual thought; school royalty didn't get initiated. Clubs initiated. All Blonde Squaders and Elites and school royalty belonged to school clubs. It made the school happy for students to be in service organizations, mostly for status and show. The school administration tuned a blind eye to the titled cliques like Elites, Blonde Squaders, Ath-Elites, and school royals, despite their bullying, narcissism, and snobbishness. Due to their parents having money and clout, they were at the top of the school's caste system.

Startled, Astrid reacted to the statement. "Since when do we initiate? And in particular, people like Cassie?"

The statement was rude, but it needed to be said because everyone was wondering.

"We never said *initiation*. We said *test*. *Life* is a test," Paloma said.

"Yeah, you also said it was entertainment," Jes pointed out. "The Christians were fed to the lions, and it was called entertainment."

"Nothing wrong with entertainment," Tish said. "Daddy paid for all this so y'all could get your kicks and I don't see anybody complaining. Now everybody grab some punch—it's got diesel—and meet me in the back. Cassie, come with me."

Hundreds of kids converged, and Jes wondered where they all came from. She bobbed her head, searching for Jester among the crowd as they pushed out of the Haunted Room into the Mystery Room, which had been locked until that moment.

Britney tried to catch up with Paloma, but all the moving bodies and Paloma's billowing gown prevented Britney from orbiting close. Tish flanked her and Britney asked, "What is in the Mystery Room and what's that got to do with Cassie?"

Tish's laugh sounded like shattering glass mixed with a witch's cackle. "That's why it's called a Mystery Room, Britney. But I will tell you there's 512s and weed if you want it."

Another reason Tish and Paloma's parties were so popular, not a parent in sight and no danger of getting busted for drugs like Oxycodone and Percocet - the 512's.

The crowd filed in, chatter and giggling smiting the air as partiers clutched red Solo cups, their faces flushed and their steps slightly unsteady. Despite the subdued lighting, the room glowed brighter than the rest of the building. It was a hotel recently purchased by Tish's father, intended for a gut and revamp and a soft opening in 2016. Some kids were lighting up, others downing drugs with a booze chaser.

"Settle down," Paloma said. "Now, when you came in tonight, you were promised a mystery guest. Everyone knows Cassie Cronrad. Give it up."

Polite applause mixed with snickering spread through the crowd.

"You were also told to write down on a piece a paper–provided to you, and pens, so there's no excuses to not have done so –the name of the student you'd like Cassie Cronrad paired up with tonight. Y'all shoulda put it in the box at the door. If you hadn't gotten a chance, now's the time to cast your vote," Paloma explained, extending a shoebox (which once housed her Stella McCartney Platform Brogues) for the slips of paper, then passing off the box. LaDonte Gaste, a gorgeous black basketball player who exclusively dated popular white girls, including Paloma, Tish, and Melody, picked through the slips and read each aloud in an undertone.

Britney interrupted. "What? Wait a minute, Paloma. I never saw anything about this!"

"Facebook and IG. Board the clue train, Brit," Tish said.

Britney and Jesamean realized they had missed this somehow. They also hadn't seen the box by the door where the votes were supposed to be submitted.

"Come up here, Cassie Cronrad," Tish said.

Cassie, despite her size, floated up, brimming with excitement. "Ya' ready for your challenge?"

Cassie nodded, the buns on the side of her ears looking slightly ridiculous, not realizing their droop had made them more like giant headphones than Princess Leia.

"All right, 'Weeners," Paloma said, drawing laughs by abbreviating "Halloweeners," "LaDonte Gaste, and Chaney Smith, my team, have tallied the votes. What say you, gentlemen?"

"Twenty percent wanted Cassie paired with Devon Amstead," LaDonte announced.

The crowd reacted with hoots and hollers, with Devon looking relieved to be in the lower percentile.

"Twenty percent wanted Cassie with Jorge Ortega," Chaney said.

More cackles and shouts erupted, and Jorge seemed equally relieved to have not been chosen.

"And the winning vote? Sixty percent wanted our buddy—Jester JR Pynes!" LaDonte announced, grinning.

Cassie's cheeks turned crimson, and both Britney and Jes stared over at Jester. Astrid leaned in and whispered something to her half-brother, who nodded. The kids surrounding them clapped and yelled.

Jes asked Jester, "Did you know?"

She gave him an accusing stare.

Jester shrugged one shoulder. Like maybe yes, maybe no. But his green-gray eyes glinted with anticipation.

"Now what?" Britney asked Paloma, who answered, "Now the fun begins."

Tish said, "Jester, come on up and be Cassie's dream date."

Jes grabbed Jester's sleeve. "What are you doing?!"

"Giving your girl the night of her life," he answered.

Jes hissed, "You go up there and we're over."

"You don't mean that. Just chill," Jester reassured Jes with a kiss on the cheek.

"What are you doing, Jesse? You don't even like Cassie," Britney said, heading him off at the pass. He tried to swerve around her, but she wasn't having it, grabbing his wrist, and adding, "You better not hurt her."

"Wouldn't dream of," he said, shaking off Britney's hand and stepping toward Paloma and Cassie.

Jes's phone vibrated, and she read the message with a frown.

Britney joined her at her side. "What's happening here?"

Jes said, "Astrid texted me. Jester told her that this is just all a big joke."

"I've heard that one before."

"Look, Brit, I know you think I was out to get Jester from you. But all that at Homecoming was supposed to be a punk. But when he kissed me, and we both felt the electricity, I lost my head."

"And your best friend," Britney said.

"You wouldn't hear us. We both, me and Jester, we

both tried to tell you."

"Tell me what, Jesamean? That y'all wanted each other so badly that you were willing to stab me in the back?"

Jes shook her head, wanting to say more but Paloma interrupted, commanding everyone to be quiet.

"Well, Jester, you've been selected by our esteemed royal students as Cassie's partner in crime for tonight. You up for this?" Tish asked, and Jester did a one-armed fist pump, the crowd roaring.

"And you, Cassie, agree to our little test?" Paloma asked, the attention laser focused on Cassie, which thrilled her and also made her face flame as red as her hair, and she nodded.

"So, Cassie. We — the Blonde Squaders and Elite women — asked you last week, some personal questions. Like, for example, 'what bug strikes terror in you?' And you answered, 'cockroaches,'" Tish said.

A couple of girls shuddered in agreement.

Cassie's eyes darted around. "You're not gonna *Fear Factor* me, are you?"

Tish tittered. "No, of course not. It's Halloween and it's supposed to be scary, but we're not gonna have gross bugs crawling around in here!"

"Man, I shoulda' brought some hissing roaches," Ian, a senior, joked, causing a few guys to blow air through their teeth, imitating the sound of the insects.

"I gotcha your roach right here," Hill, a junior, called out, holding up the end of a joint.

"No roaches," chimed in another eleventh-grader, "but plenty of cocks."

This comment set off a spattering of rooster calls. Jes used to feel embarrassed by such behavior, but now she simply sighed. Despite their status as school royalty, some of the athletes lacked class.

Britney rolled her eyes. Cassie turned scarlet, and Tish and Melody giggled.

Paloma said, "Well, you know Paloma likes her plenty," prompting the boys to cock-a-doodle and chortle.

Jes eyed Paloma, who was in a much better mood today, particularly in the days leading up to the Halloween party. Following Homecoming, and even at her own party that weekend, she had been in a foul mood. Losing the Homecoming Queen title still bothered Paloma and reflected in her cool tone when speaking to Jes. Perhaps that's why Paloma didn't tell Jes or Britney about inviting Cassie. But what was the excuse with Astrid? She was a seminal member of their school royalty group, along with Paloma, Tish, and Melody. If anyone seemed displeased now, it was Astrid. She had been excluded, treated like Cassie.

Astrid jerked her floor length fall, the long wig she'd painstakingly pinned in place, from under the bear-sized heel of basketball player Gabriel Diaz.

As an apology, he offered her some Ecstasy, or Molly as they knew it, which she promptly popped into her mouth before grabbing his cup quickly and downing the contents.

It had been a night of surprises all around. Britney had never known Astrid to take drugs.

Well, it was Halloween and maybe Astrid just wanted to have some fun.

Astrid wondered if she could forgive her friends for keeping her out of the loop. She figured it was because she was Jester's sister, and he was dating Jes, who used to be Cassie's best friend. Paloma probably didn't want Astrid to have advance warning of whatever was about to happen. Astrid had known Paloma for a long time and had witnessed how her eyes sparked fire when she was crossed, of how her jaw tightened when deciding someone's payback, and the way her lips pursed when she delivered a soul-stabbing come back, so she understood when Paloma planned things "just for fun." But Astrid couldn't understand what the deal with Jester was. He claimed to have no idea why he was chosen as Cassie's "date," but as school royalty *and* a senior, pranks were to be expected.

Jester now stood next to Cassie as Paloma said, "And Cassie, you also shared with Tish and me another personal thing. You said you'd never been kissed by a guy."

Cassie's cheeks infused with crimson, her head dipping as hoots erupted from the crowd. She then raised her eyes, appearing on the verge of tears, and said, "Paloma! That was private! That wasn't for you to blab it to everyone!"

Britney pressed her hand to her mouth, feeling mortified for her friend who'd been put on blast in a big way.

"Come on, honey, it's no big deal. We've all been where you're at, although I can't even remember that far back now," Paloma said.

"The difference between you and us," Tish said, "is that we didn't necessarily get the best first kiss or partner. But *you* will."

It was just dawning on Jes what this meant.

CHAPTER TWENTY

Jes shot Jester a look and shook her head, but he smiled and shrugged. Sliding his phone from his pocket, he raced his fingers over the keyboard. She received a text from him saying, "It don't mean nothing. It'll be over soon."

Paloma said, "Okay, Cassie, it's time for your test. Jester, it's up to you to give our friend here an experience."

Jes prickled as a vile energy shot through the crowd, who weren't there to just celebrate Cassie's enlistment into the Elites or to witness a tame little kiss. Their eyes intense on Cassie, like spectators at a blood sport, snapping selfies and content, and awaiting the loser girl to take the first blow.

Jes inched closer to Jester and Cassie, studying them. Jester persuaded Cassie to wrap her arms round his waist. He rested his hands on Cassie's love handles since no way due to her size could he cinch her in an embrace. With the crowd chanting "Go! Go! Go!" Jester leaned forward, pressing his lips to Cassie's. Her cheeks turned sunset pink, brightening her freckles until they looked like measles.

"So sweet!" Paloma patted her heart.

Jester whispered something to Cassie, and she nodded, initially looking down but then meeting his gaze.

"Awww, she's shy!" one of the Ath Elites called and

his bros laughed.

"Tongue, tongue, tongue!" Chaney Smith yelled, getting the crowd going.

Jes knew Jester wouldn't go that far. This was supposed to be a "charity" kiss, requested by Paloma. Anything more intimate was reserved for Jes and Jester alone. And the other stuff they did now, Jes no longer a virgin, and in love. The thought had no more swept through, than Jes's eyes widened, as she watched Jester coach Cassie, adjusting her head and their bodies until they were pressed together, his hunky pecs sinking against Cassie's fleshy rolls. He guided Cassie's lips with his and ran his tongue along her gums.

Jes knew the tongue action was amazing since she had experienced it. But Jester wasn't supposed to do that with Cassie.

Britney knew the tongue action was amazing, having experienced it. But he wasn't supposed to have done this with Jes, and especially not with Cassie.

Jes's ears buzzed with the cheers from the crowd, and her blood pressure rose. Cassie and Jester were totally soul-kissing! How dare he! How dare he do this to Cassie!

Britney approached Jes from behind and said, "Some joke, huh? Funny Ha. Ha. LOL. How does it feel, Jes, to have the joke turned on you?"

Without turning around, Jes said, "Screw yourself, Britney."

Britney chortled.

"No, Jes, that would be screw over like you and Jester did to me."

Paloma interrupted their exchange. "Who thinks the happy couple should have some privacy?" The crowd chimed in with "Yeah, yeah" and calling for more PDA.

Paloma nudged the couple into the same small space where Britney had been in earlier with Baron. Jes blocked Jester, who was holding Cassie's hand. "What are you doing?" Jes spat.

Ignoring her, Jester pushed past Jes. Jes then grabbed Cassie and said, "You realize you're being used?"

"And you're not?" Cassie snapped back, leaving Jes with her mouth wide. Jes's blue eyes blazed as Jester and Cassie disappeared behind a closed door.

"We have to stop them," Jes said to Britney.

"*We*? Like someone stopped Jester and you?" Britney snapped. "Anyway, you gonna stop a whole room?" The kids catcalled, all pumped up.

Jes tromped toward Paloma, crying, "End this now!"

Paloma said, "Jesamean, no can do! Your bestie wants this, Jester is willing, and we just can't barge through a locked door. Give those kids a little moment, okey dokes?"

Jes's stomach churned as she witnessed everyone in the room recording Jester and Cassie's actions on their phone.

Britney jerked on the door handle, but it wouldn't budge. "Cassie, come out! We can all see you!" The room erupted in boos. Cassie either didn't hear Britney or didn't care, staying put.

The crowd clamored with rallying cries and chortles, their eyes set on Jester and Cassie's live performance on camera, capturing every moment with eager anticipation.

Jes paled beneath her Harley Quinn makeup. Jester was feeling Cassie up and she was letting him! Cassie groaned as Jester's hand disappeared beneath mounds of flesh, his mouth doing damage along Cassie's neck.

Britney found Astrid, her near naked body posed. "Astrid! Can you get this to be over?"

"Cassie and Jester are willing parties."

"No, Cassie doesn't know about *this*," Britney argued, pointing to all the phones in the room, lit up and videoing.

"Yeah, but Jester does."

Britney blinked at Astrid, who despite being high, Britney knew was telling her the truth. "He can't stand Cassie! Why would he do this?"

Astrid tugged her long blonde wig from beneath her armpit, detangling it and it tumbled to her ankles. "Senior pranks. What can I say?"

"But you didn't know until tonight that this was going to happen?" Britney asked.

"I swear I didn't. But I do know that there is something else coming."

"What?"

"Paloma and Tishy's schemes. Do I need to say

more?"

Britney's shoulders sagged. More humiliation in store for Cassie, and not a thing she could do about it. She witnessed everyone posting Cassie and Jester's escapades to Snapchat and IG.

Jes could not stomach another minute and marched over to Melody. "You're probably the most reasonable member of school royalty. Can you get Paloma to get this over with?" Jes said.

Melody nodded, considering the compliment. "Sure, but do you really want to start a near riot?"

Just then, Jester asked Cassie if she wanted to go all the way and Paloma screeched, "Eek! Bet Jesse ain't carrying Trojans and sure don't want him to be Cassie's baby daddy!" She waddled over in her big gown and banged on the door until Jester cracked it open, grinning, while Cassie's cheeks were blood-red, her neck sprouting with egg-plant colored hickeys.

Applause exploded, and the couple joined the others. Cassie still seemed unaware that her first base experience had been captured on everyone's phones, courtesy of Paloma's stealth video recording, complete with audio.

Jes was certain she'd never wipe those sounds from her mind, sloppy tonguing and Cassie moaning in ecstasy.

Britney was certain she'd never wipe the images from her mind, Jester sucking on Cassie's throat, his fingers working her.

"So how was it?" Tish called to Cassie, whose complexion radiated bright rose, but who grinned.

The crowd was chanting, "Cassie! Cassie! Cassie!" and all the booze and snacks Jes had ingested threatened to resurface. Cassie believed she had achieved popularity and passed some innocuous tests to become school royalty. She might even think Jester genuinely liked her and that she had a chance to be his girlfriend.

Britney inserted herself between Jester and Cassie. "Cass, I have to talk to you. Now."

"Don't ruin this, Brits," Cassie said, her drooping Princess Leia buns now resembling a weird beard under her chin.

Paloma steered Cassie away from Britney and Jester. "You ready for your makeover, girlfriend?"

Cassie's head bobbed in excitement, and she followed a dozen Blonde Squaders and Elites into another room. The livestream continued, playing out on everyone's phones, and the crowd eagerly anticipating the next happening. This time, Astrid joined them.

Britney wondered if Astrid was in on it, after all. Perhaps Astrid was lying about this entire situation. However, Britney noticed all the cosmetics laid out on a table, along with a makeup mirror and chair. Astrid had been enlisted to give Cassie a makeover. Astrid gestured for Cassie to sit, but she squirmed to fit her bottom into the chair, spilling over the sides.

School royalty laughed at the sight. Jes wondered

why this crowd found watching Cassie being made up so fascinating, thinking it would probably be dull.

Some kids wandered off in search of more alcohol, drugs, and fun things to do in the haunted house.

However, Jes's heartbeat pitched as a thought struck her. Could Cassie be put on display once again?

Astrid spritzed primer on Cassie's skin, then sponged on foundation.

Jes tried to reassure herself that Astrid would fix Cassie up, just like she had done to Jes. It was a legit makeover. It was going to be fine.

However, Britney zeroed in on Cassie's bright eyes and giant grin and gauged that the crowd was less pumped as before when Cassie and Jester were making out, but still the excitement seemed way too ratcheted for a mere makeover.

A dozen kids who had left earlier, were back on the scene, whispering and giggling.

Once Astrid plucked Cassie's eyebrows, which had never been plucked before, she began darkening the carrot-colored brows. Paloma whispered something to Astrid, who straightened, resulting in a heated exchange that no one could hear but everyone could see. Paloma's face beseeched Astrid, while Astrid's lips pulled into a slash. She continued applying product over Cassie's lids, and at Paloma's instruction, Astrid dipped the makeup brush in a pot of loose shadow, this time not tapping off the excess. Paloma gestured. More, more. Astrid flung the long wig behind her in irritation, her lips tightening at Paloma and Tish's input.

The kids who returned were drunk. Although the makeup mirror had been turned away from Cassie, each time Astrid layered more application, the crowd cheered. A few of the girl's cried, "She be pretty!" or "Bless her heart," like they were their southern aunts. Red plastic party cups overflowed, kids got louder, and the smell of weed was suffocating.

Jes wanted to leave more than anything, but she felt compelled to stay and witness the outcome of this spectacle, much like a rubbernecker at a train wreck.

Jester mingled with his bros, engrossed in watching the footage of himself and Cassie on their phones. He had tried to talk to Jes, but she had flung his hand away and stomped off.

Britney also wanted to leave more than anything but had to stay there to see this thing through with Cassie, knowing how much this meant to her. Even though Cassie had made mistakes this evening, starting with accepting the invitation, then agreeing to the Blonde Squad's test, Britney got it; she'd been there herself. But her transformation and her first kiss - with Jester - hadn't been experienced in view of a thousand peers.

Astrid swept carmine lipstick across Cassie's mouth, the color as bright as brake lights. Jes thought it was too overpowering for Cassie's white complexion and ginger freckles, but Astrid had darkened her brows and lashes. Jes figured that to fit in with the cliques, Cassie would be told to dye her hair deep red, which was Jes's natural shade. She wondered, were they trying to turn Cass into *her*, just as they had turned Britney into Paloma, Tish, and Melody.

"Wow," Paloma breathed, "Cassie, you're something!"

Tish and a few other Elites whispered behind their black-tipped nails. Astrid's face pinched up as if she were constipated, which was not how she'd looked after transforming Jes.

"Let me see, let me see!" Cassie cried, clapping like a five-year-old on Christmas Day.

Except it wasn't Christmas. It was Halloween and a time for all things scary.

Every phone in the place was lifted, ready to capture Cassie's reveal.

Astrid handed Cassie the makeup mirror, and her face contorted, then she began weeping.

"What have you done to me?" she cried, but it wasn't tears of joy.

The room exploded in laughter when Cassie spun around.

"Astrid?" Cassie screamed.

"I'm sorry," Astrid said, her face stiff and her lips pulled down at the corners.

But Paloma, Tish, and all the school royalty girls did not seem as contrite. Only two other faces in the crowd remained stone-faced – Jes and Britney.

"But...but...you said you'd give me a makeover?" Cassie cried, her tears streaking the spackle from her cheeks.

"It is. We just never said what kind!" Paloma cackled like the mean witch that she was. Cassie hadn't been glammed up; she'd been clowned up. Periwinkle shadow caked across her eyelids, purple eyelashes curled like a dead spider's legs, tomato red blush slashed her cheekbones, and green eyeliner resembled a garden snake trailed beneath her eyes. Black mascara on her bottom lashes splayed like jazz hands. The only thing missing was a red clown's nose, but with all her crying, the tip of her pugged nose had already turned primrose.

"You're a jackass and a half," Britney said, grasping Paloma's forearm.

"I'm the Head Boss in Charge, Brit, and don't you ever forget it," Paloma snapped coolly. "Now get your talons off me."

Britney's palms loosened. Noticing the activity around her, she said, "Y'all better not be posting that!"

A couple of senior boys taking photos of Cassie said, "Too late. Done."

Britney couldn't hear Jester and Jes's conversation over by the corner, but witnessed Jes's blue eyes hot as flames, poking Jester in the chest with an ebony fingernail.

He grabbed her hand and pushed it away, his brows furrowed.

Now some of the people filming Cassie were pointing their cameras at the squabbling couple instead.

Cassie continued blubbering. One of the school royals said loudly, "Awww. Sad Clown."

"Leave her alone," Britney snarled. "Or I'll make you a Dead Clown."

The Blonde Squader clapped her jaw shut, she and her other friends making a hasty retreat.

Britney said to Cassie, "Come on. Let's get that off your face." She gently touched her shoulder.

But instead of taking Britney up on it, Cassie growled, "Don't touch me, traitor!"

When Britney jerked back at the rebuff, Cassie said, "You knew they were going to do this and you couldn't even warn me?"

"Cass, I had no idea the Elites and Blonde Squaders were gonna do this!"

"You and Jes betrayed me!" Cassie continued yelling like she hadn't even heard Britney.

"Cassie, listen to yourself! Jes and I would not do that to you! And if you had told us Paloma had invited you, we'd have said it was probably not in your best interest!"

"I just wanted what you and Jes have!" Cassie bawled, her nose snotty, wiping it on her sleeve. "I just wanted to kiss a guy, to have a boy like me!"

Jes appeared, Jester-less and overhearing the conversation. "Cassie, I'm sorry this has happened to you, but Jester does *not* like you. But you don't like him either!"

"Or do you?" Britney asked, her eyes widening, the realization dawning.

"Oh, are you freaking kidding me?" Jes cried. "You *do* like him! Have you always?"

Cassie's cheeks, where the caked-on foundation had been wiped clean by her scalding tears, inflamed. "You've both had your chance with him! I just wanted the same!"

Britney and Jes stared at each other. Poor Cassie! There would *never* be a chance for that. Everyone knew it but Cassie!

"Cass, I'm sorry. But Jester is still my boyfriend," Jes explained.

"Not for long, Jesamean," Cassie said, her lips pulled tight.

"Okay, I mean, we did have a fight, but we didn't break up."

"You will. He's agreed to meet me," Cassie raised her chin defiantly.

"What? No, Cassie! He's not meeting you because he likes you! He's doing all this as a joke! If he says he's gonna hook up with you, it's to carry out this prank for senior year!" Jes said.

"You did it to Britney, now I'm gonna do it to you," Cassie retorted, her Princess Leia buns messed up and frizzed out like she'd stuck her finger in a light switch. "Steal your boyfriend. Screw y'all over like you did to me!"

"Cass, Jester will either meet with you, and he and his buddies will have a good laugh, or he'll stand you up."

Britney tried to get her to understand.

"So, you don't think Jester could be into me? He said that he was," Cassie said.

"He said what Paloma and Tish told him to say!" Jes exclaimed.

"So, then you knew what they were going to do tonight?"

"No, but I know Paloma," Jes answered. "Neither me nor Brit knew about this prank. Or Astrid, as far as I can tell."

"How can that be? Astrid is one of the top chick Elites in school," Cassie said.

"Right. But Paloma is chief Blonde Squader and queen of all school royalty. She's at the top and handing down orders," Britney said.

"Yeah, she's the one who called me personally to invite me. I was so flattered. She told me there would be a special guy here tonight. She told me I'd get a makeover, just like my friends Britney and Jes. She said there would be a test. I hadn't expected Paloma to make me the butt of her joke. But…I've had worse happen to me. I guess it was worth it if it got me into the clique. I mean, I finally got kissed, and the guy wants to see me again."

Jes and Britney shared the same look of horror. After several beats, Britney said, "Cass, once and for all, Jester is using you for a prank. Everyone knows all seniors try to outdo each other. And let's be clear, this was not a test for you to get into the Blonde Squad or the Elites. Paloma never had any intention of letting you in."

"So, I got humiliated for *nothing*!" Cassie screeched, all eyes turning toward her and everyone ready for round two of the evening's drama. "Y'all will all pay! I mean it! You won't get away with this! Especially you and Jes," Cassie added, her eyes aiming a fiery glance toward Britney.

"Okay, let's just go," Jes said, trying to lead Cassie away, but Cassie nimbly shook Jes's arm from around her shoulder.

"I'll see y'all in hell," Cassie said, ignoring the catcalls from the other kids as she waddled away. "I mean it. I'm gonna haunt you. Not a Halloween haunt. I mean really terrify you!"

"With that face," one of the seniors laughed, "you did it, baby girl!"

No one was surprised when Cassie flipped him off.

But everyone's hearts stopped when all the lights went out, even the sallow bulbs, and then screams erupted. No one heard Cassie's cries as she was dragged into a blackened room.

CHAPTER TWENTY-ONE

"Shhh," the male whispered, clapping his hand over Cassie's mouth to silence her screams. He released his hand, and she asked, "Jester?"

"Yeah."

"What's happening?"

"With the lights? Probably Paloma and Tish's idea of scaring everyone, Halloween style." He already knew that "Mike Myers" (Leon Letrie, an Ath-Elite enlisted by Tish) was stalking everyone in the Mystery Room. The kids had been warned that if they used their phones for either light or to call out, that they would be "killed." That meant "stabbing" them with a rubber knife, a prop from the school's theatre department that spritzed "blood," a combination of dish soap, corn syrup, cocoa powder, and food coloring, on impact.

"I can't see one inch in front of me. And I left my phone in the car."

"Here." He opened his iPhone 6S Plus and hit the flashlight icon. "Better?"

If anything was scary, it was Cassie's makeup, dimly illuminated by Jester's phone. She resembled a female Pennywise. Her blue and black makeup smeared across her eyelids, her rouge like a bloody wound, her red lips slashed and makeup glubbed under her chin, the cakey gunk painting her as a deranged clown.

"Why did you grab me?" Cassie asked.

"Didn't want you to get hounded any more than you have."

"Brit and Jes said you did all this to show off for your bros. To move up in the senior prank's leaderboard."

"I'm not the bad guy here, Cass," Jester deflected. "Paloma asked me to kiss you. I thought you knew. I didn't know it was gonna turn into something to be streamed." He lied. But Jester needed to regain Cassie's trust to secure his position as the leading senior prankster. That meant completing Cassie Part II.

Cassie narrowed her clown eyes at him, wanting to believe him. "Really? You never liked me before. Now it's all different?"

"No, Cassie, you didn't like *me*. I wanted you to, for Brit and Jes's sake, so we could all hang out in peace." That part was true.

She nodded. "Then you meant what you said back in the Haunted Room?"

Jester had said a lot of things, so he wasn't sure what she was referring to. Nevertheless, he replied, "Yes."

She sucked in her breath, so it must have meant something to Cassie. "Then, I've made up my mind. I want to."

"Oh, good," Jester said, rubbing her back. He hadn't expected Cassie to whip around and nuzzle his cheek with her smeared clown face.

"You were my first kiss. I want you to be my, you know, *first*."

It took a beat. Well, he'd been several girls' first — including Britney and Jesamean and wasn't indifferent to servicing all three best friends (former best friends). However, he was aware Tish was live streaming this on her YouTube channel. The lights had probably been restored, and everyone had been redirected from the Mystery Room to the Devil's Den, where a big screen would play whatever happened between him and Cassie. Everyone inside would witness it.

The dusky room was now illuminated with sallow-colored lights. "You sure you'd rather not wait? Or go out to my car?" He wanted to at least give her some privacy, even though he could imagine his bros groaning if he denied them the chance to voyeur him and Cassie.

"We can lock the door, right?" Cassie asked.

"Umm," Jester said, turning the lock, as if that made any difference. Everyone could still see and hear what was happening. "But wouldn't you be more comfortable in my car, or take some time and set it up?"

"Like a date?"

"Sure."

"No, I've made up my mind," Cassie said. "I'm with you now. I want it to be now. But you could still take me out, right?" Her eyes pleaded.

Jester almost felt bad, but then he remembered how Cassie had badmouthed him to Britney, even when he had been nice to Cassie, taking her places, spending money on her. She had tried to break them up. Then he didn't feel too terrible. "Yeah, we can do that," he said calmly, but he was lying between his teeth.

"That will be awesome. But…you're broken up with Jes?"

He had no idea if they were still together or not. And if he went through with this, it would certainly be over. When it came down to it, did he want to be the senior who'd pulled the most awesome pranks before graduating? Or did he want to stay with Jes? A girl he'd never had so much in common with and could see a future with.

But here was this pathetic, needy girl asking him to do her. Fat or not, ugly or not, his body responded, ready to give her a good time. "Jes and I are done with."

"Oh, okay. You left Britney to be with Jes. You're leaving Jes to be with me."

Uuhh. What? No. This was a one-time thing. A hit it and quit it. Jester made some indecipherable noise, and Cassie said, "It's okay. I'm fine with whatever we can have together. I love you."

Jester rubbed his forehead. When did this happen? He'd never shown any interest in her, never breadcrumbing, and at best, this was a situationship. This was going to be a courtesy copulation, and nothing more. Ever. This prank was getting too complicated. He just wanted it over.

Cassie wanted this moment to last forever. But they

still had the future.

"Oh, well, thanks for that. Okay, so how do you want to do this?" Jester said.

"You're the one who knows what to do," Cassie said, a little stung that Jester didn't at least say he cared for her, too.

"I meant, we can try it on the floor, or maybe up against the wall?" He was beginning to see that the mechanics might be more difficult than he had envisioned. He couldn't pick this chick up and have her wrap her legs around him. While she was deciding, he discreetly angled his body and slid on a condom he'd gotten from one of his bros at the last minute.

"Maybe the wall?" Cassie suggested.

His testosterone spiking, he was good to go. Didn't matter that he was not attracted to Cassie in the least. Only mattered he was gonna get off, and that he amplified his prank pulling.

"Umm, I'm not taking birth control. And will we have to worry about blood, or...?"

"Got it taken care of. And maybe. But don't worry, I got you. Can you put your back against this?" Jester asked, guiding her against the wall, a place where he could purchase leverage. And it would be a good shot for the video. He only hoped he'd be able to do this. He never intended to be a porn star. He was afraid she'd drop and slide down, and no way could he prop her up.

"Can you get your underwear off?" he asked.

"Not wearing them," she said, in a voice that Jester figured she was trying to be sexy.

But no.

"Okay. Here, let's get this out of the way," Jester said, pushing Cassie's costume to the side.

She helped him, then grabbing his hand. "Could we…kiss and stuff before we do it? I mean, whatever couples do?"

They weren't a couple. Jester hesitated for a few seconds. "Sure." He kissed her like he had done in the other room, and another room where everyone was ogling them from now. He wondered if Jes and Britney were there. He hoped they were mad enough that they had left already.

Cassie was into it, this time French kissing Jester. He returned it with as much enthusiasm as he could muster. He kneaded her breasts, which were large, just like the rest of her, and at least those did excite him. She groaned, kissing him back. He placed her hand on his crotch, and she exhaled. Her touch made him forget it was Cassie, imagining it was a hot girl. Like Jes.

He was ready. She breathed heavily like she was ready. It was at a fever pitch. Just as he was about to stamp her vCard, screaming pieced the air and the door breached like the S.W.A.T team had been called in.

"Cassie, no!" screeched Britney and Jes, one of them yanking her clothes in place to cover her breasts, the other shoving Jester out of the way.

Jester flung the dry condom from his junk and zipped up.

Cassie, flushed and confused, cried, "What are you doing?!"

"They can see you, Cass!" Britney shouted. "They can all see you!"

"We're in a quiet dark room! You and Jes are so jealous of me and Jester that y'all say anything to screw up my chance at becoming a woman!"

"Elites and Blonde Squaders and school royalty, they – we – can see everything that y'all were doing," Jes explained. "We told you they were using you. That Jester only wanted to rack up his pranks. So, this would've been his ultimate!"

"I don't believe you. Jester likes me!"

Britney opened her phone, the video playing out the Jester/Cassie show, and Cassie's eyes went wide, staring at Jester, then crying. "How could you do this!"

Jester almost said he didn't get to do anything but wasn't about to incur the wrath of three females out for blood.

Paloma and Tish rushed in. "Well, thanks a lot, Jesamean and Britney!" Tish cried.

"You completely ruined the second part of Operation Cassie," Paloma accused.

"And with everything we did for you, Brit," Tish continued. "And Jes too. Getting y'all accepted into school royalty."

"Cassie isn't your prank project," Jes said, "and

neither are we."

"You wouldn't be anywhere without us," Paloma snapped. "Loser girls until we got y'all doctors and hairdressers and makeup artists!"

"Maybe. That doesn't mean you have any right to set someone up to hurt them!" Britney said.

"That's where you're wrong, Brit. Your loyalty is to *us*, not fat ugly girls!" Tish spat, either not caring or not seeing Cassie wince.

"My loyalty goes to whatever is right!" Jes said. "And none of this is! From having a party for the sole purpose of using someone to rack up prank points is just wrong! And enlisting my boyfriend in this, is unforgivable!" Jes directed her cold blue eyes toward Jester.

"Yeah, let's get this straight, Jes. Jester enlisted *us*," Paloma said, smiling smugly.

"Is it true?" Jes said from between clenched teeth.

He didn't answer, suddenly enamored with his phone. It was supposed to be a great prank. No one was supposed to get hurt. He thought Jes would get it. He hadn't expected her to side with her former best friend(s). And Paloma was only half right. He'd enlisted her to punch up his pranks. She and Tish were the ones who came up with the Cassie idea. And then asking if he could get Cassie to go to first base. He never expected Cassie to declare her love for him, or to say she wanted him to be her first.

"You wrecked the prank, sisters. You gotta bunch of p.o.'d kids in the other room," Melody said from the sidelines, then Jes and Britney saw Astrid for the first time.

"Oh, are they gonna beat us up?" Jes asked, and Tish laughed.

"Worse. Along with some dope video of Cassie, they'll post about y'all on IG and Facebook. They'll scald you," Paloma said. "Nobody likes traitors or killjoys."

Jes stared past her. "We tried to get you to go with us, Cassie. This time, we're all leaving together."

Cassie didn't argue, sniffling as she, Britney, and Jes filed out and were met with jeering.

Astrid remained mum, the only one not screeching at them. When her brother threw a glance at her, she turned her face away.

Her expression of disappointment in him was louder than all his buddies' cries of "Attaboy," and claps on his shoulder.

CHAPTER TWENTY-TWO

The Monday following Halloween, the Ghouls and Goblins Bash dominated conversations. Social media buzzed with it, and whispers filled the hallways of Manatee High, from the losers, stoners, and dweebs groups to school cliques. Jester earned the title of prank king, Cassie was now labeled "open" (despite not going all the way with Jester), and Jes and Britney got lambasted for messing up the Cassie prank.

Cassie, who was usually taunted for being ugly and fat, endured laughter as the girl who Jester had felt up, but didn't get the cookies from. Some of the Ath-Elites passed by her, offering to finish what Jester hadn't been able to. Others yelled, "Hey, Cassie. Nice rack you got. Can we see more? Or is that only for your boyfriend Jester?"

Rix Kestro, a star soccer player who'd been at Tish's Halloween party, derided Cassie, saying, "Yo, Princess Leia, wanna see my light saber?" His teammates cackled and Cassie lowered her gaze and waddled and pushed through the wall of people in the courtyard.

At the royalty quadrant, Jes and Britney faced a chilly reception. Paloma audaciously uploaded the video(s) of Cassie, beginning with the kiss from Jester, her makeover, and eventually their interrupted intimacy. Tish openly badmouthed Jes and Britney for interfering, while Astrid, unusually quiet, observed them while flipping her long black hair to one side and her spikey thick fake lashes blinked like *brisé* fans.

Jes and Britney stuck together, only because they had no one else. Even the outcast Cassie had rejected their friendship, believing Jes and Britney had conspired against her.

Jes shot a sharp glance at Jester, whom his friends surrounded, jacking him up with compliments and getting slathered with attention from a few female admirers. Although Jester hadn't hiked up his body count, his half-sex with Cassie would become legendary.

"So, are we out?" Britney asked Astrid in an undertone.

"I'm not sure. School royalty is livid. Clique loyalty is key. Paloma and Tish will chew y'all up and spit you out before you're in good graces."

Britney and Jes had been outcasts their whole life. Now they were outcasts for a different reason. "So, we're expected to toady up?" Britney asked.

"At least for a little while," Astrid said.

"And what if we don't want to?" Jes asked.

"You know the answer to that. Pariahs are usually forgotten when the next big crap storm happens. Someone will get pregnant, overdose, get locked up, and y'all will be yesterday's news. The muckrake will blow over. But if you challenge Paloma and Tish..."

Astrid let the statement dangle in the air, the

screaming nearby cutting off any further conversation.

Cassie, who'd cowered all day at the gossip, leering, and laughing at her, had finally found her voice and started screeching at Jester across the courtyard. Within seconds, they were surrounded. Paloma, Tish, Melody and two dozen Blonde Squaders, and Elites on one side, Jester's bros, and Astrid, Britney, and Jes intermingled among the lower castes of the school.

Every phone was raised, capturing videos of the confrontation. Cassie alternated between crying and shrieking at Jester, some of her rantings becoming indecipherable. "You think you can get away with this, Jester? You'll regret the day you screwed me over!"

"Cassie, I'm sorry you didn't enjoy our kiss." Jester's tone was smooth and honeyed, far from an apology, but an attempt to de-escalate Cassie's psycho outburst.

Cassie blinked for several seconds. "I enjoyed it up until I found out you had used me!" Tears flowed down her face, punctuated by hiccups. "Until I figured out the makeover wasn't for me to join the Elites, but to become the school joke!"

"What do you want from me?" Jester asked, prompting one his bros to suggest in a stage whisper, "Give her the wood!" followed by explosive laughter.

"You think I'd let you finish what your started?" Cassie squawked.

Without thinking, Jester stuck his fingers in his ears

to block her bellbird-like bellowing.

Cassie erupted like a bottle rocket. "You piece of crap! You gonna keep on dissing me?"

Britney and Jes grinned at Cassie's gumption, but she misinterpreted their amusement and yelled, "More pieces of crap! You were all in on it!"

Jes and Britney shook their heads, and Jester tried to calm Cassie, but she wouldn't hear it. Her caterwauling echoed across the courtyard, catching the attention of the resource officer who came round the corner. "Y'all won't get away with this!" she continued.

"Cassie, chill. If you get us in trouble, you'll be in it yourself. We'll all be hauled to the principal's office," Jester stated, his eyes darting to the school cop, who trotted across the length of the courtyard toward them.

"You'll wish it was only that," Cassie spat. "'2001, 'You'll Be Sorry,' the Steps. Listen and learn."

Britney and Jes knew that Cassie loved classic rock. They didn't think the group was a metal band, but they weren't sure.

Everyone was staring at Cassie who they already thought was weird. Even the musicians, who'd know Ozzy, Zeppelin, and AC/DC, Cassie's favorites. Jes and Britney liked the 90s-2000s boy bands, and of course, Britney's namesake, Britney Spears. But The Steps, not a group that Cassie's friends were familiar with, so they made a mental note to look up their song.

"I made the kiss happen. Tell me *you're* not sorry," Jester said.

"You're going to feel my pain," Cassie said, singing it, so Britney and Jes assumed this was something to do with the song. "You prick!" She added, which Britney and Jes figured wasn't a part of the lyrics. "For all your lies, let's see you get yourself out of what's coming to you!" Cassie's sea-foam eyes flashed, both beautiful and terrifying at the same time.

"What's that mean, Cassie?" Jester asked, noting the fire in her glance.

But all conversation was lopped when the resource officer pointed his baton at the corralling students, who then scattered, moving out of the cop's way. "Everything okay here?" he asked, anticipating an evasive response and knowing he would have to replay back security cameras to see what had transpired.

He homed in on a heavy girl with the bloodshot eyes – either from crying or smoking weed, who seemed to be the center of attention, and she finally said, "We're fine. No problem here."

"Good. Now get to class," he said, and the remaining crowd dispersed. The obese girl hung back, accompanied by a few others recognized by the resource office as Homecoming Court kids. Given their status as school royalty, he let it go and continued with his rounds.

"You mighta scammed me one time, Jester. But you won't again. You'll never pull another prank again,"

Cassie spat in an undertone. "Got me?" she added, adopting a gangsta-like attitude.

"Yeah. Sure, Cassie," Jester said. "Whatever."

Jester's nonchalant response only intensified Cassie's rage. Her cheeks turned fire-engine red, and then she smiled.

At Cassie's scary grin, resembling a demonic smirk on a Jack-o'-lantern's face, it scrubbed Jester's own smile from his face.

CHAPTER TWENTY-THREE

Giggling, the girls duck into a blind spot from the security camera, between the C Wing wall and the senior's lockers. All the students knew it was a blind zone – it was where the school drug dealers exchanged Molly and weed with their buyers – why didn't the school administration?

"Did you see their faces?" one girl asked.

"Yes! Did you hear them scream? Telly Richards almost choked on her gum!" the other girl said.

"This prank is going to go down in school history!" the pretty blonde grinned.

"I know! Jester blew his Operation Cassie final phase, but this'll definitely put us in the running," the second blonde said, shifting her gun. "Even if we're not seniors yet, we'll make our mark before then."

"Are y'all sure we aren't gonna get in trouble for this?" the third blonde asked. Even though they had timed their prank for eleventh grade Biology, right before lunch period, when the teacher wasn't in the classroom yet and students weren't expected to have their devices in their backpacks upon entering, that didn't mean some random person could have gone rogue, calling the law on the "gunmen."

"Do you want to become legends or not?" the first girl said, adjusting her mask and tucking wisps of blonde hair under.

The third girl didn't notice her question had gone

unanswered. She continued, "I mean, couldn't we get arrested for this?"

"If we got caught," said the second girl. "Which we won't. Anyway, these guns aren't even real." The weapons looked convincingly authentic and could fool even experienced firearms handlers.

"I can't believe how easily we got the outcast to go along with this," the first girl said. "They were all in when I told them we could one-up Jester. They wanted to give it to him good for the whole Cassie thing. It was more important for what's - their -face to screw Jester over than it was for them to retaliate against us."

A few seconds elapsed as the girls adjusted their masks and wedged tightly into the dead spot.

Biting her bottom lip behind her mask, the third girl spoke up, "Where are they? Are you sure they understood the plan?"

"Nem's a loser but not stupid," said the first girl.

"Should we text 'em?" the third girl asked.

"No! We want as little digital stuff as possible! That's we spent so much time in person going over this, instead of posting on FB, Skyping, or Face Timing," the second girl said.

Then they heard crying and clumping coming toward them, the "gunman" barking orders.

"They're coming!" the first blonde whispered, her eyes gleaming behind her mask.

"It's go time," the second girl said, grabbing the forearm of the third girl. "You can do this, right?"

The girl nodded, her stomach cramping as her friend pulled her out of the blind spot and into the open.

"Hurry, they can't get to The Morgue before we do!" the second girl said, hastening.

"We got this! POA has already gone down," the first blonde said, scrambling around the corner towards the auditorium/The Morgue.

Then they heard two things that weren't part of the Plan of Action – the unmistakable noise of multiple shots, sounding like real bullets, and sirens, possibly arriving sooner than the girls had anticipated.

CHAPTER TWENTY-FOUR

Jes, who had been in the girls' bathroom, barfing up her breakfast and cursing the lingering flu her doctor said would last only a few days, but now knew the symptoms would probably not run their course soon. She snapped her head up from the toilet bowl at the sound of the gun blasts. It was not some innocent commotion in the halls or seniors setting off firecrackers by the girls' lockers. As a member of the Trap Shooting Squad, Jes recognized the noise of gunfire. An active shooter in her school! She automatically reached inside her pants pocket for her phone, only to realize she had left it in the classroom.

Where to go? Her mind raced. She could hunker down in the bathroom, lock the door, and stand on the commode for a semblance of safety. But she knew that wouldn't be foolproof if a shooter burst in and peered under the stall. Recalling her training on school massacres and Manatee High's protocols on lockdowns, she tried to stay calm and focused.

Shivering, she regulated her breathing while cautiously skimming along the wall, as if teetering on the edge of a precipice. Inch by inch, she scooted toward the bathroom door, peering outside with one eye. Just a few feet away was the janitor's closet, one of several scattered across different wings of the school. Janitor Bates had occasionally left it unlocked, either for convenience or by oversight. Jes remembered the seniors raided it last year, stealing supplies for their pranks (of course, toilet papering everything in sight). While it was likely that the janitor had learned his lesson and latched it since then, Jes couldn't stay holed up in the restroom, nor could she reach the designated safe place in the auditorium, where everyone was supposed to go if they weren't in their classroom when lockdown occurred.

She bolted from the bathroom just as there was an explosion of screaming down the hall, triggering a yelp of her own. She gripped the doorknob, eyes widening as it gave way, and she burst into the supply room. Both Bates and Jes gaped at each other, the janitor engrossed in his M3P player, blaring George Strait and defying the no-smoking rule on campus with a cigarette dangling from his lips. Jes couldn't care less about his rule-breaking or his potential anger at her intrusion. She ripped the earbud from his ear and blurted: "Someone's shooting!"

He clenched his cigarette between two fingers and said, "Are you helping the seniors with their pranks, Miss Homecoming Queen? Gonna try to steal my cleaning stuff?"

"This is not a joke! Call 911 right NOW!"

Noting the chalkiness of her face and the tremor in her lips, Bates swiftly grabbed his phone and barked the address to the 911 operator. After he'd hung up, Jes said, "I need you to unlock the Armory." The Trap Team stored their firearms there, even though guns on the rest of the campus were strictly prohibited. Many squad members brought their personal weapons to the nearby Manatee Sports Complex for practice sessions.

"The police will be here soon."

"It took SWAT over forty-five minutes to respond at Columbine. Twenty minutes after the 911 call at Sandy Hook," Jes hurled back, familiar with the stats. The public scrutinized law enforcement's delayed response times in those cases. "Dozens could be killed in that amount of time!"

"Only the Trap Coach and campus safety can unlock the Armory Room."

"Do you see any resource officers around here?" Jess cried. Unbeknownst, he lay dying, shot by the assailant when he stopped them inside B Wing by the stairwell.

The janitor hesitated, then fished a keyless card from a large ring. "I don't know anything, understand? The seniors stole it when I turned my back."

Jes snatched the card from his fingers and sprinted down the hall toward the sports equipment storage units. Bates was worried about getting into trouble. It would be the least of his concerns if multiple lives were lost. Jes had to retrieve a Remington from the supply cabinet and ammo from a separate cabinet, then load the firearm swiftly. She skipped the protective glasses, vest, and earmuffs typically worn on the shooting range. Jes may not have been the most skilled marksman on the squad, but she had demonstrated proficiency in the field. She didn't have time to question her decision to confront the shooter; she was in defense and protection mode.

A dozen students clamored out as she neared the building, their eyes flying to the Remington. They screamed, "The Morgue! There're four shooters! They got people trapped in The Morgue!" The auditorium was The Morgue.

At ground level, several students shattered a window with a hurled desk, scrambling out, cut up from the shards, and tears streaking their faces. "No one else is in there!" yelled one of them, cradling his bleeding elbow.

Jess pressed forward like a salmon swimming against the current, disregarding the stragglers rushing out.

CHAPTER TWENTY-FIVE

The gunman marched Britney and the remaining students from her class toward the auditorium, sans Lyle, who had died in the classroom along with the teacher. Jes had escaped the chaos by being in the bathroom during the shootout. But four of her classmates were shot in the hallway when two attempted to flee, and two had given the assailant lip. Britney had no idea about Jes's whereabouts or if she had even fallen victim to the gunman.

Decades ago, Manatee High School students and teachers named the auditorium "The Morgue." It was associated with boredom, endless lectures, and principals speaking about school policies that killed kids with tedium. Therefore, it was a place where people went to die.

The three blonde accomplices jerked the doors open as they herded students inside. One of the masked blondes shouted, "What's going on?! What's with all the shooting?"

"Just giving them a good scare," the gunman assured her. "Sit down right now! These rows here. You move one inch, I'll let you have it!" The students complied, and Britney was at the end of the aisle, staring at the four intruders.

"Ooooh, you're scary and all," the blonde said. "You're good at this."

"Y'all chained the doors coming in and out, right?" the gunman asked.

"Yeah, just like we went over it. The only exit is in the back for when we make our escape," the other blonde said.

"Did someone call the police?" the third blonde asked the gunman. "We heard sirens. I'm not liking this. It wasn't supposed to happen like this. I'm not gonna get in trouble for a prank."

"Can you chill the f.o.?" said the second blonde. "This will all be over soon. No one can get out of here except through the back. No one has gotten past us, so we're okay."

"Do you think we're on lockdown yet?" the third blonde said.

"Don't know, don't care," the first blonde said. "We got Britney and Jes here; that's all that counts. And I texted Jester last night and told him to hit The Morgue before study hall was over, and I told Astrid the same, this morning, to show up."

"Except Jes isn't here," the gunman said.

"What do you mean?" the second girl asked.

"She's not here. She's been sick. She probably ditched today," the gunman said.

"No B.D. Jester and his bros will slide in any second now. I told him I had something special for him. He insisted I tell him, but I made it all sexy and mysterious, and what man can resist that?" the first blonde laughed. "And Astrid will come because I asked her."

As they whispered to each other, their guns remained trained on the terrified students. "Just like you wanted it," the first blonde said to the gunman. "All the betrayers trapped in a bubble where they can't get out."

"Even y'all," the gunman said.

The three blonde girls exchanged looks. "Hey, you're not still mad, are you?" the second blonde asked.

"Mad? No. Livid. Yeah, enraged," the gunman said.

"You mean like literally? Or just a figure of speech?" the second blonde asked.

"Literally. And you know what happens when you're authentically livid? You think about how to stop the pain. You start thinking about how to take out the ones who caused that pain."

"Right. Which is why we're including you in on this prank," the first blonde said.

"Y'all love your punks, don't you?" asked the gunman.

The question went unanswered as Jester and six of his bros fresh from 'A' wing swung the doors wide, trailed by Astrid and another Elite named Reece. They all froze when they observed the four people training a bead on them.

"What the frick?" Jester cried.

"Dude, I told you I heard sirens!" one of the bros said. But none of them had heard the gunshots.

"If we're locked down, it means other kids are gonna be coming to The Morgue, and instead of being safe, we're all in danger!" said another bro.

"That's why all the doors are chained up!" said another guy. "Because they're in here taking hostages!"

"Shut up. Hand over your phones," demanded one of the gunmen, the first blonde. She jerked her head to the third blonde, who collected them.

"Paloma?!" Jester cried. "Is that you? What's got into you?" He pretended not to have his phone on him and brushed the blonde away.

"How do you like our prank, Jester? Is it senior-ranked worthy?" the blonde said.

"Paloma? If that's you, you told me to meet you here, that you had a surprise for me," Jester said.

"And didn't I deliver?" she said, ripping off her mask and hoodie. Her two accomplices stared, and she added, "He already knows it's me. We might as well get comfy while we wait for the next batch of kids to show up."

The two other girls hesitated, then snatched off their masks and hoodies.

"Shoulda known. The terrible three," Jester said of Paloma, Tish, and Melody. "You in on this, sis?"

Astrid shook her head. "No. Why would I want to? Y'all are in deep."

"That's why we didn't tell you, Astrid. You're getting less fun as time goes by," Paloma said.

"It's called growing up," she shot back.

Before Paloma could retort, the front row of kids began hopping out of their seats, some of them chewing the Squaders out for scaring the snot out of them, while others said, "Then what we saw in the classroom wasn't real, right? So, Lyle and Mrs. Petrakowski were in on it. What an awesome prank!"

The shot had them screaming again, startling them into a sitting position. The gunman was on stage, pointing the weapon at them. "Did you forget about me, Paloma? But that's nothing new, is it? Wipe me from your mind, like I'm a turd on your perfect butt, like I don't exist, unless it's to target me, to humiliate me."

Jester and his friends and Astrid and Reece hadn't noticed the gunman until now, so focused on the conversation with Paloma, Tish, and Melody. With the gunman's size, they shouldn't have been hard to miss.

"Who is that?" Reece asked, peering at the gunman.

"Is that a real gun?" one of the bros asked.

"No," chorused the Squaders, while the gunman answered, "Yes."

"What are you talking about, Cassie!" Paloma shouted, ratting Cassie out, and she removed her mask and hoodie. The identity of the other prankster got some snickers, and others gave her props with some applause for the prank. "These are not legit. They're totally 1:1," Melody said.

"Y'all's are. Not mine," Cassie told them, and some of the students gasped.

Authentic? Then that meant that everything that happened in the classroom was real. The four kids she shot in the hall, that was real. Some of the kids started weeping.

"What are you talking about, Cassie?!" Paloma cried. "We got these online! They only look and sound like the real thing. Where would you have gotten ahold of a real gun?"

"You're kidding me, right? Just like you can go to any sketch part of town and get any kind of drug you want, you can get an assault weapon too. For the right amount of money, no background check, no ID, no waiting period."

"So how much did you pay for it? What was the price for taking people's lives?" Astrid asked.

"Settle down, Astrid. I got no beef with you, even though you cake faced me on Halloween. I know Paloma and Tish put you up to it. Maybe even your brother. Because that's what he does, he sets people up and gets others to do his dirty work, then he gets to shine like a diamond." Cassie pointed the gun toward Jester, and a few girls in the front row cowered.

"Cassie, come on now. Let's hash it out. Just don't hurt anyone else," Jester said, his tone smooth and soothing, but his left green-gray eye twitched.

"Yeah, let's do, Jester JR Ray," Cassie said, and for a second, Jester relaxed, believing he could talk her down. But then she added, "Let's talk about how you hurt me. You don't want me to hurt anyone, but you don't mind doing some damage to others, now do you?"

"I'm sorry, okay?"

"Are you now? Could have fooled me, laughing it up with your boys, posting stuff on YouTube, IG, Facebook. So hilarious how you pulled pranks on the gross fat girl, huh? Upped your senior creds. Just super rad, aren't you?" Cassie's voice dripped with sarcasm.

Jester didn't have words but sucked in his breath when he finally noticed Britney, who'd been mum all this time. "Y'all proud of yourself?" she said. "The Elites and Blonde Squaders who thought nothing of bullying and badmouthing kids? Jester, you see what you've done by pulling your pranks? And now we're all stuck in here with someone who's finally had enough," Britney said.

"Shut up, Britney. You and Jes thought you were better than me when you got accepted into school royalty. You and Jes laughing at me, who'd always had your back and always would, until you turned on me."

"It's not true, Cassie…"

"Stop lying!"

"Cassie, I know how much it hurt you for these girls to prank you at Halloween, how it hurt you for what Jester has done, but you're not getting revenge on anyone by killing innocent people!" Britney pleaded.

"Oh, you thought I was targeting *innocent* people? No, Britney, anyone I shot *deserved* it! Mrs. Petrakowski singled me out in front of the whole school at lunchtime weeks ago! McDonald's wrappers and potato chip bags were blowing around on the ground, and she assumed they were mine! She told me to pick up my trash, and when I told her it didn't belong to me, she said, 'Who else would eat five burgers and two bags of Ruffles for lunch? And it's right in front of where you're sitting.' Everybody was laughing. Then, the four kids I shot in the hall, they've all bullied me at one time or another. And I shot the resource officer, only to keep him from coming after us, but I think he'll be okay. Lyle was collateral damage. I only shot him because he was trying to call 911. But he had no trouble giving me a look of disgust anytime I passed by him."

"Will you listen to yourself, Cassie? You're not even you anymore!" Britney said, her voice wavy with unshed tears. "The Cassie I knew was kind-hearted. She'd never hurt someone and especially not like this! You, me, and Jes were all bullied at one time or another. But we didn't go after people when they hurt us!"

"You're right. I'm not myself. You know when you're not yourself anymore? When you get either teased, harassed, ignored, or shunned every day of your pitiful life. When those days add up to years of hell. When the only two friends you have leave you behind. Don't ever compare me with you and Jes! Y'all were able to reinvent yourself, ugly ducklings to swans! And when I had a chance to, you and Jes were jealous. Yes, jealous.. I knew it and cooked up this scheme with Paloma and Tish to fake-make-me-up!

Y'all got Jester to make me the laughing stock of the entire school!"

"Cassie, I swear to you that Jes and I did not plan this thing at Tish's party! We love you. We wouldn't knowingly do this to you! I'm begging you to end this now! You know there's no way out of this, don't you? If you end this now, you'll probably get leniency. They'll see you're mentally ill. But if you keep on, the police are gonna storm in here because you're holding hostages. And they'll have no problem taking out the threat!"

"Then I might as well do what I came to do," Cassie said, and she aimed the gun at Britney, whose hands splayed up in front of her face.

"Paloma," Cassie said, the assault rifle still trained on Britney.

"Y-Yes?"

"Run."

"What?"

"Run. Now!"

Everyone's eyes widened as Cassie shifted the weapon from Britney to Paloma. Paloma bolted, her legs churning up the aisle. *Pop!* Cassie dropped her, leaving her with her spine blown out, face down, and paralyzed.

"Well, I gave her a chance," Cassie said, as kids screamed and bawled around her, some of them spilling out of their seats and crouching on the floor. "Which is more than I'm gonna give you." Cassie said, turning the assault weapon on Tish, hitting her squarely in the chest, cutting off her scream within a second. The wails echoed through the auditorium, blood splattering among those sitting near Tish.

A few of Jester's bros bounded toward the side exit. Cassie's shot shattered one guy's fibula, then piercing another guy's heart in a direct hit, and the third boy's carotid severed. Jester's guttural cry caught in his throat. Astrid's hand gripped his, her fingernails embedded in his palm, but he was numb to the pain.

"Anybody else wanna try to leave?" Cassie asked, and a row of students shook their heads, tears leaking down their cheeks.

"Brit, you told me back in the classroom that I'd never shoot you. But that's where you're wrong."

"Cassie, no!" Britney cried.

"But first, Melody." *Da-dat!* Melody's guts spilled from her abdomen, and she slumped forward. Kids erupted screaming and sobbing.

"Three egotistical bullies down," Cassie said. "Two more vain ex-friends to go," she added, pointing first at Britney, then at Jester.

CHAPTER TWENTY-SIX

Jes was still reeling from the information she'd been fed, a group of weeping juniors as they sneaked out the back while Jes crept in. Their eyes enlarged when they spied the Remington, and Jes cried out, "Where is he? The gunman?" and they went slack jawed, like she was nuts. One of them whispered it was Cassie Cronrad who'd shot a bunch of people. Jes had spat: "Is this a sick joke?!"

An Elite that Jes trusted, said, "I swear it's not. She's gone seriously cray." Then, jerking her head toward the Remington, she added, "If you're any kind of friend to her, you'll put her flat line."

Jes had no time to process this – or exactly what the girl had meant *by if you're any kind of friend*. The group of kids scurried away. Jes inched her way toward an exposed section near the underclassman's lockers. She felt like a video game character in *Sniper Elite*, sneaking around hallways, walls, and corners, and prepared for gunfire with her weapon, whereas Cassie personified *School Shooter North American Tour*.

What had happened to Cassie? How long had she been planning this, and who could she have gotten to go along with it? It wasn't like she had any real friends outside of Jes and Britney. But Jes also knew Cassie had been hanging out with a new group of friends, in Cassie's words, "losers like me."

Jes just couldn't imagine that Cassie could have planned this by herself – or could she? It seemed the logistics would have been too complicated. For a fat second, Jes wondered if Cassie had done this because of a boy – for a boy. Just like Britney had fallen under Jester's spell. Just as Jes had.

Jes tiptoed past the janitor's supply closet, the door firmly shut. Maybe Bates was even locked in there, awaiting police before he came out. Coward. But at least he had given Jes the keycard to get into the Armory Room. She rounded a corner, recoiling at the sight before her. Four bodies lay strewn in the hallway. Cassie, *no! You didn't*! Jes screamed internally. Squatting, she checked for signs of life, but no heartbeat or pulse danced beneath their skin. And the other two, there was no doubt they were gone, one of them with glassy eyes, and the other's complexion waxy as fake fruit.

Jes snapped erect at the screams of terror and bawling coming from The Morgue, where students were designated to go when they couldn't access a secure room during lockdown. The auditorium was always left unlocked, and Cassie would have known that.

Jes crept up to the thick doors and pressed her ear against it. She struggled to make sense of the muffled conversation, but she could only decipher crying, then shouting. She sprang back at the sound of a *bang-bang-bang*. No! Not more gunfire!

She couldn't barge in without risking getting shot

herself. Jes realized the blast had come from an assault weapon. The Remington was no match. The kids had told Jes there were four shooters. Cassie and who else? And even though Jes's weapon might be like a peashooter compared to an AK-15, she had to try to end this.

Jes knew that even if the cops got there soon, department policy might charge that they had to wait for backup or a key to breach the locked-from-the-inside doors. All this could take time.

She knew something that cops or S.W.A.T might not know; there was a side door that led to the balcony. Unlike the area on the ground floor, the school usually kept it locked. High schoolers weren't allowed on the balcony except the nights when the theatre students graced the stage with *Our Town*, or *Alice in Wonderland*, or the like, or during daytime for collective assembly, when all four grades packed into the auditorium. Jes prayed that Janitor Bates had left the balcony unlocked as he made his way around C Wing cleaning.

She pulled on the door, and it cracked open. Silently, she shut it behind her and blended into a shadowed curtain, getting her bearings. The screams and crying from below were no longer muffled; their elevated decibels reverberated off walls and columns. Some kids pleaded for their lives, and then she recognized Britney's voice.

Jes tiptoed, then hunched in front of the balcony, where she couldn't be seen but could hear the conversation: "Three egotistical bullies down. Two more vain ex-friends to go."

Jes swallowed the gasp, shifting the Remington, as it dug her rib. Then Britney, crying, "Cassie, I'm begging you not to shoot me!"

Then two seconds before Jes stood up, Jester's voice pleaded, "Cass, I know you've been hurt by the bullying all these years. I'm sorry we pulled that prank on you. Will you forgive me?"

Cassie's face softened. "It was several pranks. But forgive you, Jester? Sure."

"That's good, Cassie." Jester let out an audible breath of relief. "That's a good first step. Now, put the gun down."

"Ahhh, Jester. Always making it seem like it's someone else's idea to do something when it's actually you all along. Smoothing up all the time. I said I'd forgive you. I never said I'd forget it."

The initial relief Jester had experienced vanished when Cassie's cheeks infused red with rage. Though her face darkened, Jester's went white, Cassie aiming at his forehead.

"Don't you dare!" shouted someone. Startled, Cassie lowered the gun and squinted, trying to locate the voice. Her eyes widened when she spotted Jes from the balcony.

Cassie took aim at Jes as she drew a bead on Cassie. Every kid in the auditorium flipped around in their seat, watching the tense standoff. Astrid squeezed Jester's forearm, her face filled with fear.

"Jes, so good of you to join us," Cassie said. "You're just in time to watch me blow away your boyfriend."

"Cass, please don't hurt anyone else! Just put the gun down!"

"You first."

"No, Cassie, I can't do that. I can't take that risk."

"Sometimes its risk versus reward. Like when I started thinking about how I would make y'all pay for humiliating me in front of school royalty, in front of the whole school, then the world when everyone posted the Halloween videos. But then it just fell into my lap when Paloma and Tish asked me to help them punk everyone. They thought it'd be so funny to scare everybody, then at the end, say, 'It's only a prank, guys!' Well, it is kinda funny. And it did give y'all a big scare. But it's not over. The fun and games are just beginning." Cassie suddenly shot up onto the balcony. Jes clutched the ground, landing hard on her weapon. The blood rushed in her ears like a raging river as her heart pounded wildly. The students erupted in screams, not just from the warning shot, but because they realized they were the next targets.

Cassie systematically shot from left to right, blasting each kid in the row. They either died on impact or were gravely wounded. Only Britney was spared, crawling under her seat and sobbing.

"You okay there, Brit? You're welcome. Lucky girl," Cassie said.

Jes leaned over the balcony, the Remington

trembling in her hands. "Cassie, I'm begging you not to shoot anyone else!" There were still a handful or more people in the auditorium who had not fallen to Cassie's siege. "If you do, I don't want to shoot you, but I will."

"You gonna go at me like I'm one of your clay pigeons? I've already done it, Jes. I got nothing left to lose." Cassie raised her voice over the cacophony of wailing, moaning, and screaming. "When you're a loser, you don't worry about what else will be taken from you. Only when you're a winner, like you and Britney, given your chances to change your life around. My life is over – whether it be because a sniper takes me out, or I go to prison for the rest of my natural life."

"Cass, if you stop this right now, even if you go to prison, you'll still be alive!" Jes shouted, tears gathering at the corners of her eyes.

"Won't that be a good time, huh, Jes? The fat ugly girl stuck behind bars with other killers, and addicts, and peddie's. Where I'll not only get bullied twice as worse than at school but beat up or shanked as well."

"I want you to live!" Jes pleaded, realizing it was true. Cassie was not a monster. She was a dear friend who'd gone off the rails.

"You think this is living?! Being teased and talked down to every day! And I could take it when you, me, and Brit were Three Best Mates, remember? I had you and Britney in my corner. Now y'all like Snapchat 'Best Friends,' erasing yourself from my life! Like I'm some

Skylar Neese! My best friends like Sheila Eddy and Rachel Shoaf killed me off." A pause.

"They don't wanna be around me anymore!"

"Yet you're the only one killing people off!" Jes cried, her fingers still gripped around her weapon. "So don't compare our friendship to them!" The 2012 national case of the two best friends killing a third best friend, sparked horror and a public outcry.

"Oh, excuse me for insulting you," Cassie snipped.

Then there was rumbling outside the building, the muffled sound of feet pounding.

It was either a mass exodus of students being evacuated or S.W.A.T teams arriving. Cassie believed it was the latter.

Hearing the noise, Jes pleaded, "Cassie, I beg you to give yourself up! To let everyone go!"

"So, you want me to give everyone here a chance to get out?"

"Yes! I'll wait with you. I'll be here when they come for you," Jess promised Cassie.

"Okay. All y'all," Cassie pointed the weapon at the remaining group of kids. "Go. Get out of here. And y'all weren't born in a barn, so shut the door on the way out."

"Thank you, Cass."

"Don't thank me yet, Jes. You, Brit, and Jester. Y'all have to stay. And put your gun down, or I'll pop them right now."

Jes hesitated, placing it on the floor.

"Kick it. I wanna hear you punt it out of the way."

Jes booted the gun across the carpeted floor, and it banged against a baseboard. "Satisfied?"

"Yep. Go!" Cassie jerked her head at the group of students.

Astrid hesitated, but her brother gave her a firm but gentle push. She and the others raced down the aisle. *Da-tung*! One student went down. *Da-Dot! Da-Dot!* Two more were hit. Two others hit the ground and rolled across the floor like they were Valeri Liukin performing triple back somersaults. A third Ath-Elite, desperate to escape the gunfire exploding around him, grasped the door handle, and Cassie blew apart his phalanges. He screamed, cradling his destroyed hand and collapsing. The door cracked, and a mysterious forearm appeared, grabbing the guy's ankle, yanking him out of the line of fire. His wails of pain penetrated the thick doors, paying the price of his freedom with some of his fingers left behind.

Astrid scrambled over two dead juniors, an Elite and a Blonde Squader.

Da-tung!

Astrid screamed, pressing her hand to her grazed face as blood spurted between her fingers and flesh hung from her cheekbone. *Da-Dot! Da-dot!* Moaning, she crumbled.

Jester's cry reverberated through the auditorium. "*Astrid*!"

"Don't move, Jester. Or I promise you it will be your last one," Cassie said.

"Isn't that what you came for?" Jester yelled, tears

crawling down his cheeks. "To kill me, Brit, and Jes?"

Cassie didn't answer, instead she shouted, "Britney, front and center!"

Britney remained curled in a ball under her seat, her long legs twisted weirdly beneath her.

Cassie screamed, "Do it now! Or I'll finish off anyone who's still alive in here!"

At least a dozen kids had perished. Moans echoed periodically from behind the seats closer to the door where some students had thumped over. If they were alive, it had to be barely. There was no sound, no stirring from where Astrid had slumped over.

Britney untangled herself, shaking as she stood. "Cass, you don't have to do this!"

"I know, Brit. But see, I want to. Now go stand over there next to your ex-boyfriend."

Jester nestled her hand in his, his trembling vibrating in his veins, his palm sweaty.

"Aww, how sweet. Like you never even broke up. You see this, Jesamean?"

"Cassie, the cops are gonna storm in here any minute. You have to give yourself up," Jess said.

"I have hostages. They're gonna negotiate with me first."

"They won't! They'll shoot first, ask questions later!"

"Then I better hurry and do the deed. So, who do you want me to kill first, Jes? Your boyfriend, or your BFF that you stole him from?"

The unanswered question prodded Cassie's sharp glance – and Jes was nowhere to be seen.

"Jesamean! You better show your face right now!"

"Sorry. I was throwing up."

"Yeah, heard you haven't been feeling so hot. Left a little gift for Bates to clean up, huh? Now quit screwing off and get over here with them."

"You sure you want me to do that? You know the only way into the balcony is through the auditorium's outside door. And if I do that, the cops will see me and not let me back in."

Cassie's forehead puckered, suspicion registering in her eyes. But she said, "Yeah, you're right. Well, that's what a balcony is for, huh? To get a bird's eye view of the show?" She then aimed at Jester, and his grip pinched Britney's fingers.

"I'll drop you if you do it," Jes said, retrieving the Remington and pointing it at Cassie.

Cassie grinned. "I'll put him down before you even pull the trigger."

"Cass, I'm begging you to stop -"

"— I told you to get rid of the gun. So, because you didn't listen to me..."

Da-tung, Da-tung!

Britney's feet flew out from beneath her. Her blood sprayed Jester, her hand entwined with his, jerking him forward. Jester's eyes were huge, his hands shaking as he fisted them to his chest.

Jes's throat was deluged with tears, and she contained her scream. She hadn't known Cassie was going to fire off. Jes peered at the carnage, wondering if this was just a dream, a nightmare where she'd wake up soon. Amongst moans and death rattles of some of the kids, she made out the scurrying along the hallways outside The Morgue. She shivered, never believing the moniker would go from pedestrian nickname to an actual charnel house. Shaking because she understood that S.W.A.T or whatever law agency was in charge, would burst in at any second and take Cassie out, in a hail of gunfire. Cold, calculated, as Cassie's own rampage. Armed Elite snipers who would kill Cassie on sight, a threat eliminated. Code 4. S.W.A.T talk for 'Everything okay. Scene secured.'

Jes wanted to flee through the balcony door to safety. But she wouldn't. So, she faced Cassie, with tears flowing down her face.

Jester's eyes flew toward the balcony, then at Cassie.

"Clean up on aisle four," she said to him, and when she trained the weapon on him, he rooted to the spot like a giant oak, not one eyelash flitting.

"You want me to finish him?" Cassie asked, and Jes shook her head vehemently, unable to speak, the rock in her throat cutting off her breathing.

Cassie ordered Jester to his knees. "If you're going to execute me, then I'll go out standing," he refused, and Cassie gave a bitter laugh. "Jester, always trying to push your rules. But I'll play along. As a matter of fact, I'll not only let you stay standing, I'm gonna let you sway."

Jester's forehead crinkled with confusion.

Then, Cassie ordered, "Get yourself going, Jesse JR Ray. Jog over toward your sister. Go!"

He ripped down the aisle and as he neared Astrid, *da-dat, dad-dat!* And he crumbled beside Astrid.

Jes's legs became leaden. This time she didn't weep. She swallowed, the cloying scent of blood mixed with a burnt scent from the weapon being fired, settling into her esophagus and she fought to keep from passing out.

"And then there were two," Cassie said, squinting up at Jes.

"There will be only one who will make it out of here."

"Yeah, should I go ahead and take it? Suicide by cop?"

"Isn't that what you planned for?"

Cassie released a bitter laugh. "Do you think this is what I wanted? I wanted to have my best friends with me forever. I wanted to be pretty, curvy, and popular. Now I'll be known for another reason, the girl responsible for a school shooting, just another Brenda Spencer, Laurie Dann, Jillian Robbins, Latina Williams, Amy Bishop."

Jes assumed these were female mass murderers. "Put down the gun, Cass. We'll walk out together. I'll tell the cops not to shoot. I'll even walk out before you, that way they'll see I'm okay and you don't have a weapon."

"We're not walking out together. One of us will be going out in a body bag."

Cassie kept her aim on Jes.

Jes's arm drooped, the Remington growing weighted, her mind heavy with grief and responsibility. Still, she kept Cassie in her sights. "Then we'll both go out in a Hefty."

"Well, I will anyway. You're more like a Small Recycling Bag, with your renewed, improved looks," Cassie grinned, bringing her sense of humor even now in the midst of tragedy. "You know, most school shooters kill themselves before they're ever taken into custody. Harris and Klebold, Columbine, Lanza, Sandy Hook, Cho, Virginia Tech, Rodger, Isla Vista. Very few are taken alive."

Cassie had done her research, but Jes knew some stats too. "But those boys in Arkansas in the nineties, the police didn't kill them, right?"

"Johnson and Golden didn't surrender, Jes. They were trying to flee and the police got them."

"I just meant, they were minors, like you. They had their day in court. You can too."

"They killed five people! I've killed more. I wouldn't go to juvy. They'd charge me as an adult. Can you believe those boys got released? Ten years. They only served ten years! That's our justice system for you. TIFU, if you ask me. They didn't deserve their freedom."

Jes didn't know if Cassie's info was correct or not. Either way, Jes didn't expect the same outcome for Cassie, who'd never see the outside of prison again.

"So, you're gonna take a shot at me because I killed your boyfriend and ex BFF? So, this is revenge now?

Then you're no different than me, Jes."

"It's not revenge, Cass."

"Then it's because you want the glory? Be the hero of Manatee High for taking out the shooter?"

"No. I'm gonna do this because I love you." Jes recalled what one of the Elites had said to her this morning. *"If you're any kind of friend to her, you'll put her flat line."* Now Jes understood. Some hell-bent snipers would storm in and blow Cassie to pieces. To be a hero. To extinguish the perpetrator. A sharpshooter wouldn't care that Cassie has once rescued a kitten from a storm drain, or that she gave her flip flops right off her feet to a shoeless homeless woman who was hobbling on a hot sidewalk. A marksman wouldn't care that Cassie had been Jes and Britney's best friend.

Cassie howled with laughter. "That be rich, my homie! She's gonna come at me because she loves me! Gee, Jes, glad you don't hate me then!"

"I want my face to be the last thing you see, Cass. Not a sniper. Not you in hand cuffs, staring out a cage. Me. My eyes looking into your beautiful seafoam green. Always thought your eyes were so pretty. Do you understand me?"

Cassie and Jess cocked their ears toward the battering, something cracking, someone shouting. Cops had breached one of the doors the Blonde Squaders had barricaded.

"You'll tell my mom I'm sorry? That I love her?" asked Cassie.

Jes nodded, a lump in her throat as tears flooded her eyes.

"You'll tell the cops that I tried to kill you. I'll shoot over your head. I promise. But you might want to duck, alright?"

Jes squeaked out an 'Okay,' the tears stinging her eyes.

"And then you'll…do it?"

"Yes, Cass." It was the last gift of friendship that Jes would ever give her.

"Bye, Jes. LYLAS." Love You Like a Sister.

"Bye, Cass. LYLAS."

"You won't miss, will you?"

"No, Cass." Jes sobbed. "Hurry!" She dipped her head, and even though she knew it was coming, the blast Cassie delivered to the back of the balcony, startled a yelp from Jes's throat. The wall was toast, the evidence for when Jes told cops that Cassie had tried to shoot her.

She straightened, aiming. Cass stood ramrod still. She squeezed her eyes shut. Jess said, "Cass, look at me. It's okay. It'll be over quick."

Cass stared into Jes's brilliant blue eyes. "We'll count down?"

"Yes. On three. I'll do it on three." Jes grasped the Remington, her eyes blurring with tears, and she blinked furiously, clearing her vision.

"One," Cassie said, stiffening.

"Two," Jes said with her, and squeezed the trigger.

Cass rocketed backwards, a hole between her

shocked seafoam-colored eyes, whether from the burst of pain, or that Jes had lied and hadn't gotten to "three" as she promised.

It was better this way. The element of surprise had saved Cassie from changing her mind or turning her gun on herself - or Jes. It was kinder to shave off time in the penultimate seconds of Cassie's existence.

Jes had just taken a life. Not just any life, not just some random crazed gunman, but her best friend. No one would know what really happened. The secrets revealed in the auditorium this day would go to Cassie's grave. And because of this, protect Jes's future.

Police burst in, barking orders, checking bodies. They slammed Jes to the floor, and the Remington was kicked away from her. "I'm not the shooter!" she screamed over and over, her arms jerked behind her back, her nerve endings burning as one of the men mumbled as he attempted to cuff her and her deformed arm wouldn't cooperate with his efforts to secure her. Two of the men rolled her and latched her from the front. "She shot at me! She tried to kill me! I had to kill her to defend myself! I didn't want to; she was my friend!"

One of them glanced sharply at the blasted wall of the balcony. "For all we know, you were one of the shooters!"

"No! No, I'm a student! I tried to stop her! Cassie Cronrad! She's the only shooter!"

"Then why do you have that gun?"

"I'm on the Trap Team! I was in the bathroom when Cassie started shooting everyone! I ran to the Armory and got the Remington. I was trying to protect everyone!"

"We got some kids here with pulses!" one of the officers reported.

Jes screamed, "Jester! Is it Jester? He's right there!"

The guy looked up and shook his head. Jes dropped her head, gulping her sob. But her head snapped up when another cop said, "This one is still breathing."

"Her name is Astrid! It's Jester's sister. Help her!" But Jes knew medical would be held in staging until the scene was secured and cleared.

Another cop tilted his head toward his shoulder, someone speaking on his radio. He called out to his commanding officer, "Sir, we got the janitor telling officers that a girl on the Trap squad took a gun to go after the shooters."

Now they had it confirmed that Jes's story was true. But at the mention of shooters—plural, the commander firmly grasped Jes's forearm, saying, "Who are the other shooters? Where are they?"

"No, there was never any other shooters! It was a prank, you see. Cassie and Paloma, Tish, and Melody cooked this thing up because of what Jester did to Cassie on Halloween! Jester had all the points for senior pranks and the Blonde Squaders and Elites were trying to pad their cred before they got to twelfth grade. They were supposed to pretend to be shooters! They had fake guns. But the Blonde Squaders didn't know Cassie was gonna do this *for real*! I don't know where Cassie woulda got a weapon from, but she did know how to shoot. And the Elites didn't know about Cassie either! I didn't know, or I could've tried to talk Cassie out of it. Or Britney could've of." Then Jes looked toward where Britney had collapsed, but she had disappeared! Jes cried, "Britney! Where is she? She was right there! She must have crawled away! That means she's okay! Brit, where are you?" and when Jes didn't get a response, she cried, "Please! Someone find her! Britney Glascier! She's tall, got brownish--mostly blonde hair and she was wearing jeans and a pink shirt."

"Miss, we're checking everyone," a cop said, bending over bodies.

"So, you're telling me this whole thing was a prank?" the commander asked Jes.

"A prank gone horribly wrong. Yeah, but none of this woulda happened if the Blonde Squad and Jester hadn't pulled that joke on Cassie." Jes stopped, not wanting to speak ill of the dead, but knew it would probably come to light during the aftermath of today.

"We're going get all the details when we take your statement, down at HQ." He had no idea what she was talking about. The only thing he understood? Kids littered the floor left and right, most dead, some injured, and this was all because of a stupid teen prank?

He shook his head. Such a waste.

"Sir, we've got the whole building cleared, that's all the students and teachers who we're trapped inside during the shootings, but it's chaos outside. Parents are screaming for their children, and the media is swarming. Everyone wants to know who the shooter is."

"No comments to the press or parents. No one gets in here but medical," the commander ordered, still grasping Jes's elbow.

"Copy."

"Can you please take these off?" Jes asked, and a cop stepped forward. Jes rubbed the wrist on her deformed arm as they unshackled her hands from in front of her, feeling her elbow had twisted uncomfortably. The commander told her, "You'll leave with paramedics."

"I'm not hurt." That wasn't true. She was injured for life, seeing all her friends gunned down. Seeing Cassie's fear in those last few seconds before she died. Knowing it was by Jes's hands.

The commander's eyes narrowed as he studied Jes. He knew from experience that many victims remain unaware of the severity of their injuries during a massacre or crime. Cassie's shot grazed Jes's scalp, the blood trickling from her hairline. The shot Cassie intended to go over Jes's head had made its purchase.

"Will have EMT's take a look at you anyway, protocol, you know," the commander explained, not calling attention to Jes's wound, which he estimated would require a dozen staples at least.

"Will I be charged? Go to jail?" Jes asked, trying to divert her gaze from Cassie and Jester's bodies.

"That's not for me to say. There'll be an investigation. Higher ups will decide if you're an accessory."

"I'm not."

"I'm certain you aren't. But we still got to piece this together." As far as he was concerned, the girl probably prevented many more deaths. But she had not gotten authorization to get the gun from the Armory, and for that, she might be in trouble. She was also underage, so hopefully it would play out in juvenile court rather than her being charged as an adult.

Paramedics rushed in. One of them began taking Jes's vitals and attending to her head wound. Some of the kids were carted out on gurneys, clinging to life. Others were stepped around or stepped over, unable to be saved. Jes averted her eyes from Cassie's lifeless body on stage. Uniform cops, crime technicians, and detectives milled about. Jes just wanted to leave. She wanted to be alone with her grief. But she understood she would be questioned once she was taken from here.

Jes noted a flash of a pink blouse as the paramedics lifted a student's arm. "Britney!" Jes cried. "I think that's Britney!" Medical continued assisting Jes, even as she tried to spin around to see if it was her friend on the ground, and she asked for the tenth time whether Britney was okay, after receiving a laser stare from the commander, a separate group of paramedics replied, "We're working on her."

Law enforcement removed Jes from the auditorium before the bodies were bagged and loaded into a large white van at the back of the building and then transported to The Morgue — a real one, where instead of multiple rows of seats, there were multiple body lockers.

With the commander flanking Jes's right and two other special crime team members, one on her left and the other clearing a path for them, they led Jes through the back exit, the one Jes had stormed through that afternoon with the Remington. She blinked against photographer's bulbs, then microphones thrust in her face and video cameras panning her. Parents screamed at her, 'Where's my child?' 'Did you see my kid?' and she charted how the sun dipped low over the trees, signaling the afternoon gone and nightfall around the corner. How long had this rampage gone on? Jes had lost track of time, her cellphone still in her backpack in Mrs. Petrakowski's room and the auditorium was the only room that didn't have a clock mounted on the wall. Most students, reliant upon their cells, even when they had to tuck them away during class, didn't wear watches. Unless they had Fitbits, and usually only the "sporty" kids, like those on the Relay Team or the HIT students.

"Are you the one who killed the shooter?" a reporter

yelled.

"Yes," Jes mumbled.

The commander gave her a look, *muffle it*. But Jes didn't want speculation, assumptions, and misinformation about what had happened.

"Did she try to shoot you?" yelled another reporter.

"Yes."

"So, you had to defend yourself?" A reporter in the crowd yelled to be heard.

"Yes."

"Did you know the shooter?" Another one cried.

"Yes. Cassie Cronrad. My friend."

"Then you know why she shot her classmates?"

Jes wouldn't reveal it was a prank. Not when parents were awaiting word on their child. That would come out later. But now, Jes had a platform.

"Bullying. She was teased and harassed and bullied for years. I've been victimized too, but not like Cassie, who got it online and in person. But Cassie…she just wanted to be accepted. What she did, it wasn't right. It should never have happened. Too many years of being snubbed though, she changed."

Jes cupped her forehead with a trembling hand, every camera capturing her emotional pain. The truth was, she and Britney had changed. Jes could blame all this on Cassie being bullied, and it was certainly a huge reason, manifesting in what happened today. But if Jes and Britney hadn't transformed, hadn't become school royalty and had stayed losers, Cassie would have never resorted to this. Their friendship had kept her in check. And snatching that friendship away, coupled with the Halloween pranks, had caused Cassie's breakdown.

"I grieve for anyone who was hurt, or worse, today. It's horrible. Shooting people doesn't make the shooter's pain go away. It just brings it to light. It just happened last month! That guy in Oregon who shot his classmates at his college! Every year, someone does it. Someone who was bullied or made felt they were nothing. It has to stop! These school shootings have got to end. Bullying kids at school and online, it's got to stop! Today, when the media reports this, when you talk about this, when people read about it or see on the news or social media, I want you to remember, this is not *just another* school shooting. It's *our* school. *My* school. Where change can start and bullying ends. I got nothing more to say." Jes's voice wobbled with exhaustion, her legs turning to butter. The adrenalin had worn off.

The commander steadied Jes and ushered her into a squad car.

Jes's mom had been at her job when she heard about Manatee High School having an active shooter. She'd been escorted by officers to HQ and told her daughter had taken out the gunman, shocking her to her core. As she sat on pins and needles awaiting their reunion, she had learned that Cassie had been the shooter. It had to be a mistake! But a police official confirmed the horrible truth. She couldn't understand it. She knew Cassie. A good girl, but a girl with an inferiority complex because of her size and looks. Just like Jesamean, until she'd been transformed, as well as Britney, they were best friends.

"Will my daughter have charges?" the mom's voice trembled, and the police official had explained it would be up to the powers - that - be, but he doubted it. If it were how agents on the scene and students were saying it happened – and they'd still have to wage a formal investigation – Jes's actions would be commended.

"Jesamean!" her mom cried, grasping her to her bosom, like when Jes had been an infant at her teat.

"Mom, it was Cassie! She shot up the school!"

"I know. I just can't understand why! Did she tell you?" Mom asked.

"The bullying. And me and Brit pulling away from her! If that hadn't happened…it's our fault!"

"No, honey. Cassie was just…she was just so far gone and none of us saw it!" Tears sluiced her mom's makeup, brown ribbons in her budget foundation, grieving Cassie and the other victims but grateful for her daughter's survival.

A detective interviewed Jes (without Mom, who paced next door as she waited), and it was then she learned that Britney had died. All the anxiety and terror she'd felt back in that auditorium came rushing up, and she screamed, her sobs guttural. Britney, Jester, Cassie – gone. Paloma, Tish, Melody – dead. And Astrid barely holding on. Investigators gave her space, her stomach rolling and her shoulders shaking as she wept. When the mewling subsided, an investigator offered a box of tissues, and she blew her nose, her nostrils and throat raw, and she proceeded to give them the details of what had occurred, before the shooting, specifically Cassie at Halloween, and what Jes believed led up to the rampage.

Every word was true. But what had transpired between her and Cassie premortem, she didn't reveal it. She'd never tell.

Someone else, though, had secrets as well.

Soon, their secrets would collide.

CHAPTER TWENTY-SEVEN

Jes had stood before reporters, cops, and the world, delivering an impassioned speech to ensure that her school's shooting not be dismissed as "just another School shooting." However, despite her fervent efforts, Manatee High's tragedy fell into that category. That's how it became labeled – "Just another school shooting," a tagline Jes despised and could never escape.

While sadly school shootings had become common place, the Manatee High Mass Killings stood out in three significant ways. First, unlike the typical mass shooter profile – predominately male and usually White –Manatee High's gunman was a White female. Experts attribute biological factors to gender disparity in mass shootings. With their higher levels of testosterone and slower development of the prefrontal cortex, males often struggle with self-control and exhibit more aggression. In contrast, females have greater blood flow to the prefrontal cortex, enabling better intuition and self-restraint.

Although Jes suspected that Cassie suffered from mental illness, the medical examiner discovered that, much like males who display violent tendencies, Cassie's brain exhibited decreased activity in the prefrontal cortex and focal abnormalities in the left temporal lobe—all of which are associated with aggressive behavior. The abnormalities and signs of overall brain dysfunction pointed to mental decline exacerbated by years of bullying and humiliation.

Secondly, while most school shooters either die by suicide or get taken down by cops, a student neutralized Manatee High's gunman. What made it even more incredible was that a female civilian took action and had been friends with the shooter. This revelation had deemed Jesamean Marcos, once an ordinary student, as a hero and a voice for bullied students. She received admiration and sympathy from all sides.

Thirdly, Jes had become the only Homecoming Queen in American history to eliminate a school shooter. Her unique status as a queen with a visible deformity – an arm she had worked hard to conceal along with a prominent birthmark – was exposed to the world. Despite her reluctance, Jes became an example of resilience in the face of bullying. Her journey showed that inner strength transcends physical appearances, as the emotional and physical scars from her deformity had a more profound impact on those around her, even though her makeover had eventually transformed her into someone outwardly beautiful.

The press, parents, cops, and survivors hailed Jes as "brave, beautiful, and selfless." But Jes believed there was nothing brave about putting a hole in her best friend's forehead. It was a matter of kill or be killed.

Taking someone's life, especially a friend's, was an act of selfishness.

Was Jes beautiful? Perhaps, with layers of makeup masking her cheek and the areas where the wine stain bled into. Some might argue Jes was beautiful despite the birthmark, citing her flawless complexion, bright blue eyes, high cheekbones, and thick auburn hair as extraordinary features. However, Jes was well aware that without Astrid's help, she would still be a bullying target. If she and Britney hadn't transformed from bullied losers, perhaps Cassie wouldn't have spiraled into darkness, and she would still be alive – and countless others.

Despite her qualms, Jes agreed to be interviewed by local press, *Orlando Today*, and national morning television shows from the top agencies, appearing on the Big Four. Although everyone was already familiar with the details surrounding the Manatee High School shooting, Jes chose to recount the moments that led to her taking Cassie's life. Her voice remained strong and confident, carrying the weight of her narrative. Yet, amid her retelling, she carefully guarded her private conversation with Cassie in those final seconds before the siege ended.

Regardless of Jes not feeling like a hero, the public deemed her actions lifesaving. Consequently, all charges against her, including unauthorized access to the Remington out of the Armory, were dropped. Cassie's mother, despite her grief, commended Jes for her quick thinking. On television, Cassie's mother acknowledged that Jes had been a frequent visitor to their home, deeply aware of Jes's pain in having to take Cassie's life. She highlighted Cassie's mental illness and the support Jes and the late Britney had provided. Although the major networks sought to interview Jes and Cassie's mother together, they could not. In a private moment, they embraced each other, tears streaming down their faces as Jes pleaded for forgiveness and Cassie's mother whispered, "Of course, honey."

Jes became the spokesperson for the newly developed PEER campaign (Prevent-End- Expose-Report – School Bullying & Violence), a joint effort by local businesses and the school board. Jes became the face of youth activism against school shootings and initiated supportive measures. The platform provided Jes with a purpose and outlet for her grief, temporarily distracting her from her own hidden truth. But soon, she knew she would have to confront it. The burden of guilt and the secrets between her and Cassie were overwhelming. But this other profoundly private secret would get revealed soon, no longer something she could hide. Jes hoped that, just like her heroic image, people would perceive this truth as an act of bravery and perseverance.

Amidst the development of her public persona, Jes almost believed in her own fabrications.

However, someone who was intimately familiar with her saw beyond the façade. When they eventually revealed their own truths, Jes's carefully constructed bubble would shatter, leaving her exposed and wounded.

CHAPTER TWENTY-EIGHT

In the aftermath of the Manatee High School shootings, the lives of thirty-seven people were lost, including two teachers (Mrs. Petrakowski, and Mr. Bonnen, a math instructor who'd tried to stop Cassie in the hallway), thirty-four students, and Cassie. The students Cassie killed were all members of school royalty. They'd also previously bullied Cassie. Another seventeen individuals suffered injuries from gunfire, some requiring weeks to recover. The campus safety officer survived, but three students faced life - altering, permanent injuries: an eleventh grade Elite with brain-damage, a senior Ath-Elite and star basketballer who became quadriplegic, and Astrid, who endured a shattered jaw and cheekbone, and partial paralysis.

For two weeks, the halls of Manatee High remained silent, except for Janitor Bates and a few volunteers who bleached and scrubbed the blood-stained floors and walls. In front of Building C, the chain-link fence jangled as someone placed teddy bears or flowers in remembrance. Thirty-six photos with captioned names and/or grades stared back at the mourners (Cassie's was not allowed).

The school replaced the pre-massacre less-than-sturdy fencing in the parking lot and campus with military-style installations. The school also erected metal detectors at all points of entry into the campus, resembling hulking robots. Some mourners expressed discontent with the safety measures, deeming them too little too late and likening the newly erected fencing to a prison.

More than half of the student body – as well as fifteen faculty members --had dropped out. Former Manatee High students enrolled in other schools or pursued homeschooling or GED options, leaving some to question the point of the safety measures that had recently been initiated.

GoFundMe accounts helped defray the costs of multiple funerals over three weeks at a rate of approximately eleven-thirteen per week. Surviving students attended on different weeks, based on their emotional strength.

Except for Jesamean Marcos, no one attended all three weeks of funerals. Despite her mother's concern about the emotional toll, Jes felt compelled to. Britney and Jester's funerals during that first week, shattered Jes.

Cassie's funeral was held on a cloudy and cool afternoon, two days after the rest of the Manatee High students had been laid to rest. Among those in attendance, Jes was the only Manatee High student present, accompanied by Cassie's mother, an elderly aunt, and Cassie's mom's employer, making up a small gathering of four. Against Cassie's mother's wishes for a burial and a visible grave, Cassandra "Cassie" Anne Cronrad was cremated, following a detective's concerns about potential grave desecration. As they exited the funeral home, protestors and haters shouted at them, validating Cassie's mother's decision.

Leaving the funeral home, Cassie's mom patted Jes on the shoulder and said, "I know it's hard, but try to keep your appetite up. You look so drawn, dear." Jes nodded, unable to find the words to speak. Guilt weighed on Jes for being unable to comfort her in return, but she felt emotionally drained and lacked the energy to do so.

Jes channeled her remaining energy into PEER and safeguarding her secrets. Immersed in her role as an anti-violence advocate, Jes leveraged her commitment as a reason not to return to Manatee High. The school and community gifted her despite not attending, however. She readily embraced privileges typically reserved for seniors, including exemptions from having to complete specific classes, the ability to complete her graduation requirements online, and various academic opportunities. And just like that, she had a full ride to a four-year university, courtesy of a scholarship. The burden of maintaining a high GPA or working to support herself through college vanished. Now, her primary concern was choosing a major to ensure financial stability. Although the disparity of receiving these opportunities while many tragically lost their lives weighed on her, Jes expressed profound gratitude for the chance to build a promising future.

The principal personally thanked Jes for sacrificing herself to save so many others on November 24, 2015, and promised to do everything within his power to prevent such a tragedy from happening again. Internally, Jes shuddered. She'd never say it aloud but wasn't sure if all the safety measures in place would effectively prevent another incident. She believed the best prevention lay in anti-bullying campaigns, but teaching self-defense became crucial if that failed. And there lay the irony.

After the November 24th shooting, Manatee High's Trap Club membership skyrocketed. When Jes and Jester were part of the club, there were only thirty participants. Now, enrollment had swelled to two hundred students, including homeschoolers and students from other high schools lacking a club.

This trend extended nationwide, where Jes emerged as a symbol of responsible gun ownership and a defender against armed threats. Principal Wordell approached Jes, requesting her to assume the role of president of the trap club or at least attend their practice sessions to inspire others and showcase her shooting skills.

Jes regarded herself as a decent marksman, not on par with Jester or some of the other team members. Nevertheless, she reminded herself that her capabilities were sufficient when it truly mattered — when she took down Cassie. The memory sent shivers down her spine every time she dwelled on it.

Renewed interest in gun instruction sparked

protests and outrage, but they did not target Jes. Nevertheless, it affected her – the debate centered on "Gun handling will promote more mass shootings," versus "Proper gun handling will foster better self-defense and discourage school violence." Jes didn't know if it was an oxymoron or paradox; she didn't concern herself with semantics, the politics surrounding guns and adolescence, or the NRA funding for scholastic sports shooting. She declined offers to be a spokesperson for trap shooting teams but continued advocating for PEER. However, the revelation of her latest secret might jeopardize her position as mouthpiece for PEER, and she feared it.

CHAPTER TWENTY- NINE

At Astrid's house, Jes wrapped her arms around her friend tightly, the expensive perfume Astrid wore pleasantly wafting around her as always, but with a medicinal smell as well. Jes fought from wrinkling her nose at it. The iodoform-ish odor seemed out of place around Astrid, her ordinary scent ambrosial and pretentious. Perhaps it emanated from her bandaged face, concealing Astrid's horrendous injuries and scarring. Unconsciously, Jes touched her own face, hiding the port wine stain beneath carefully constructed makeup.

"I'll be popping wheelies in no time," Astrid said, locking her wheelchair in place as she faced Jes on the settee.

"I'm sure," Jes said, too brightly. "We could post a pic of you doing a stunt and me hanging off the back."

"Yeah? I think you've pulled too many stunts as it is."

Jes sat back, puzzled by Astrid's comment. Did she mean something about Cassie? About PEER? "I was trying to cheer you up."

"Oh, were you?"

"How about we get a few photos together? Put 'em on Snapchat, IG?"

"Like I'd want anyone to see me like this."

"I didn't mean to upset you, Astrid. I thought you wanted me to come over. I've tried to see you a few times, but your parents said you didn't want company. I mean, I get it.. So, when you texted me, I thought it would be okay to hang out."

"Like it was old times?"

"It won't ever be like that. We can only go forward."

"Yeah, I've seen you on TV, on your socials. You've had no trouble moving forward. Meanwhile, some of us are stuck in a wheelchair."

"There's no chance you'll…get better?"

"You mean walk? Very slim. Possibly after years of rehab."

"That's good, right?"

"In the sense I'm lucky to be alive and only partially paralyzed?"

"I'm sorry, Astrid. But yeah, because so many others didn't make it."

"I don't need you to tell me who did or did not make it."

"I miss Britney and Jester, too." Jes said, purposely avoiding mentioning Cassie.

"Do you, Jes?"

"Can you just tell me why you're so mad?"

"Oh, so many reasons, Jes. Let's start with my friends being dead, my legs not working, and my face being messed up and needing several plastic surgeries, which still might not restore me to where I was before."

"I'm sorry, Astrid. I hope you can walk again someday. And I lived with a messed-up face and a deformed arm for years. So, I know that pain. But

Astrid, you're still beautiful! You'll get the surgeries and get better."

"Oh, Little Miss Ray of Sunshine." Astrid faked a big smile.

"I know you're going through something, Astrid. I am too. Not like you, but my own personal pain."

"Because you killed your best friend?"

"Yes."

"But Homecoming Queen still got to be a hero. Still gets endorsements, followers, and a platform." Astrid ticked off these points on her chipped, peeling fingernails. Jes felt surprised, having never seen Astrid without a perfect manicure. Or her hair dyed black. With Astrid's natural brown hair peeking through her black scalp, it gave her a weird hot roots, ombre look.

"I didn't take any money from those. I'm trying to prevent more shootings, stop bullying, and break this cycle."

"Heard you got a full ride for college though. So don't tell me you're not prospering because of this shooting."

"Astrid, it wasn't about financial gain. But I'll take it. Because unlike you, my family doesn't have the means to send me to college."

Astrid seethed in anger. "Well, my family might have the money to send me and my younger siblings, but now I can't go. You know of any campus that can truly handle someone like me with paraplegia? And don't tell me to look online or ask on my FB. I can't think about going to college. I can't even finish high school at this point. Not when I got PTSD, too."

Astrid's dilemma put Jes's snippy attitude into check. "I understand. I also have PTSD, but I've got to take advantage of this scholarship."

"Of course. It wouldn't do for Manatee High's Homecoming Queen to miss out on college. Like she was a common loser. Oh, right. That's before I transformed you. Think you can do me the same solid?"

"So, you think I don't deserve any of it because I didn't come by it naturally?" Jes instinctively pulled her deformed arm closer to her protectively, a nervous habit.

"I don't think you deserve any of it because of Cassie," Astrid said, causing Jes's chin to drop, her eyes shut tightly.

How Jes wished it hadn't ended the way it did. But more people would have been shot if she hadn't killed Cassie. "It wasn't how I wanted it to end."

"Seems to me, it's *exactly* how you wanted it to end."

"Astrid, do you really think I wanted Jester, Britney, and Cassie to die?" Jes's blue eyes narrowed with pain.

"I heard you. I know the truth."

Jes's stomach plummeted, although she had no clue what Astrid was referring to. It felt like something prophetic was about to come to light, something that would change everything.

. "About what?" Jes asked.

"I know several things. But let's start with Cassie. I heard you and Cassie. In The Morgue."

Jes's mind raced, trying to connect the puzzle pieces, but she couldn't make sense of it.

"When I was lying there, pretending to be dead, so I wouldn't get shot again. I heard you and Cassie. But you thought I couldn't hear. You saved yourself by killing Cassie."

"I killed Cassie because she would have gone after more kids, even cops!"

"If you hadn't have killed her, she would have been captured alive. Would have been put on trial and spent the rest of her natural life in prison where she deserved to be."

"So, you wanted revenge? And would that have brought back Jester, Britney, or any of the Elites?"

"You set yourself up for being the champion. Congrats."

"I never wanted any of this!"

"You made Cassie believe she had no other options. Such a good friend, aren't you Jes? Let me blow your head off Cass. Let me kill you with love, instead of these cold hard cops who don't care about you," Astrid accused, taking fragments of conversation, mixing fabrications and truth to create a distorted reality. Jes wondered if Astrid's intermittent consciousness had muddled her understanding of what happened in the auditorium.

"So, I should have let some SWAT guy get the glory for taking out 'just another' school shooter?" Jes drew quotation marks in the air.

"You and I know Cassie wouldn't have survived one day in prison. So yeah, as much as it slayed me, I'd rather Cassie die from my hands than someone else's."

"Yet she and Britney wouldn't have done the same for you."

Was Astrid suffering not only facial injuries and paralysis but also brain damage? Jes stared at her for several seconds before saying: "I don't know what you're talking about."

"I know. That's what's so tragic, Jes. The pranks the Elites and Blonde Squaders planned? It was nothing compared to what Cassie and Britney tried to do."

Jes's brain buzzed like a swarm of locusts. "Paloma, Tish, and Melody conspired with Cassie to pull off this supposedly biggest prank Manatee High had ever seen. To top Jester's. But Cassie had her own ideas. The Elites thought they'd get one over on Jester, but they had no clue Cassie wanted to get back at them for the whole Halloween thing. Britney couldn't have imagined."

"No, Jes, it was *you* who couldn't have imagined. That your two best friends would have screwed you over left and right."

Jes sank back into the sofa. "What does that mean?"

"You were too trusting, Jes. Different than Cassie, who should have never trusted Paloma and Tish Halloween night. So, it isn't surprising you missed the signs."

"Signs?"

"From the beginning. You can't possibly think you can steal your best friend's boyfriend and get away with it. That you can become beautiful, and get Homecoming Queen, and not ruffle feathers, especially Cassie's."

"I'm sorry that I wasn't there for Cassie like I should've been."

"Yeah, I'm sure you are. But she found what she needed in Britney."

Jes cocked her head. "I'm not sure she did. And I never set out to steal Jester from Britney. Jester and I vibed early on. Besides his physical attraction to Brit, I'm not sure they ever had anything more than that."

"Well, you've taken from him more than Brit ever got, huh?" Astrid said.

"What do you mean by that?"

"Like I said, Jes, did you really think Britney was going to let you get away with taking Jester from her? Then, when the Elites and Blonde Squaders decided to put a plan in action to use Cassie, it was a done deal. Unfortunately, Cassie didn't let Britney in on her plans to kill off the school royalty."

"You're saying Cassie *and* Britney were planning to shoot up the school?" Jes asked in disbelief.

"The Blonde Squad enlisted Cassie. They didn't know though that Cassie was going to turn the tables on them. They didn't know Britney was part of her plan. And just like Cassie put one over on school royalty, she fooled Britney too."

There was a satisfied look on Astrid's once pretty face.

"How do you know this? And why didn't you stop it?" Jes asked.

"I didn't know until after it was all over."

"I don't believe you! Britney and Cassie, conspiring against *me*? Is that what you're saying?"

"You don't have to believe me, Jes. I can show you."

"On social media?"

"No, by texts and recordings."

Jes stared. Astrid held up a familiar phone case with the initials JRP. A lump formed in Jes's throat. Jester's phone! That meant Astrid had seen her messages to him. That meant she *knew*. "How did you get it?"

"When he got shot, he fell, the phone right next to him. As I lay there faking death but thinking I was for real dying, I scooted it to me and put it in my pocket bra. No one knows I have it, not even our parents, 'cos when they came to the hospital, I was in a gown, but the hospital staff had just bundled all my clothes in a bag and handed them to my mom. I think they even forgot the bag was in the car. I had to ask them what had happened to my clothes that I had on that day, and Mom looked kinda guilty and then found the bag and gave it to me without checking the clothes, which were ruined, but the phone was still inside the bra, so then I had to figure out Jester's password. When I did, I went through his phone." Astrid's eyes glinted but she gave nothing away.

Jes finally said, "You'll let me see it?"

Her look was hard.

Astrid opened it and scrolled then, seconds before handing it off to Jes, said: "Britney had sent him a bunch of texts. The usual break up angry ones. Then one said the biggest prankster in school was going to knock Jester off the leaderboard. She never said it was her. But she made it sound like it was the Elites and Blonde Squaders. So, Jester wasn't alarmed about it. Knowing him, he was probably amused. You know, Jes, what he and the school royalty did to Cassie was not cool. But he had no idea how that Homecoming kiss was going to backfire on him. He didn't get that "a woman scorned" thing. You know that saying. But then he had two scorned chicks, both Cassie and Brit. He never knew that those two would conspire against him."

Jes leaned in to palm it, but Astrid held it just a hair out of her reach. "You know you really threw a monkey wrench in the plan, don't you? Britney thought Cassie would go down for the plot, letting her take out Jester and you. But you were sick that morning. They thought you'd left school to go home. No matter though. Taking out one of their targets was enough."

Jes grabbed the phone, leaving Astrid helpless to retrieve it. Curiosity and anger flooded Jes, overpowering any sympathy she should have felt for Astrid rooted in her wheelchair. She read the messages, scrolling through thousands of stalker texts Britney had sent, and then her own desperate messages to Jester. Jes looked up, meeting Astrid's gaze. "This isn't incriminatory. There's nothing about Britney and Cassie working together. There are also texts from Paloma and the other Elites. They mostly talk about wanting Jester to meet them in The Morgue."

"Paloma worked her stuff right on up to the end. She and Jester had sex the day before the school massacre. She wanted to make sure when she dangled that carrot in front of Jester, he'd hop to it like a hungry rabbit."

At Jes's pained expression. Astrid added: "Oh, Jester couldn't stand Paloma. But he didn't mind using her. He thought he was making gains with his pranks. He didn't know Paloma had her own game. You shouldn't take it seriously, Jes. Those two have been hooking up long before Jester and Britney were a thing."

"So, Paloma and Tish transformed Britney, so they'd have her on their side? Or was it just 'talent scouting' the competition?" Jes asked, attempting to piece everything together. "Because they already knew Britney had that outrageous body, was already getting eyelock from guys. Maybe they were jealous but were keeping their enemies close?"

"All that."

"And that's why you transformed me?"

"Maybe. But I also liked you, Jes. But who could've known turning ugly ducklings into swans would have led to the deaths of so many."

"So, what next?"

Jes tried to make her voice sound matter of fact. "Are you gonna turn Jester's phone over to the cops?"

"The cops already have so many kids' phones, including Britney and Cassie's. I'm sure they don't need any more 411 on what happened. But guess what, Jes? I not only have my brother's phone, I also recorded as much as I could on my own. Unfortunately, because of glitching, there's no video, though I'm sure you'd want to see it all played out again, huh?"

At Astrid's cutting remark, Jes shot back, "For someone who thought they were dying, you sure got busy, didn't you?"

Astrid snickered. "You've been busy yourself, huh, Jes?"

Jes pulled her deformed arm toward her and didn't answer.

"Evidence of Britney and Cassie banding together is there, even though it's not spelled out to anyone. You'd have to read between the lines. And I have a clear recording of you and Cassie's convo."

"Okay. So, what now?"

"So now we wait for the bomb to drop."

"Which is?"

"Come off it, Jes. I read ALL Jester's texts. The ones he sent to Britney on the day she and Cassie had planned to do this shooting. But it was too late. She couldn't reel Cassie back in. Jester knew there was something wrong and suggested Britney and him to get back together again so he could smoke her out. But Britney also didn't know Jester and Paloma had smashed. Or that you and Jester had exchanged all those texts, pleading for his help, confronting him, pregged up like *Juno*."

"I didn't expect it either," Jes said softly, catching a tear drop and brushing it away. "We had talked about a future, maybe me following him to college after my graduation. But a child wasn't in his immediate plans."

"Yeah, I see that," Astrid pointed at the texts aimed at Jester. "My brother musta been overwhelmed! First, Britney's millions of calls and texts berating him about you and y'all's relationship but then wanting him back. But you didn't know that. Then, all your calls and texts panicking about the pregnancy and asking what Jester was going to do about it. Then Cassie's venomous texts and phone calls!"

"I didn't know anything about Brit and Cassie," Jes said. "I was focused on me. Here they'd told me at the doctor's I had a persistent strain of flu. They didn't even give me a pregnancy test. But when my period was late, I figured it out. I did two home tests to be sure. Then I told Jester the tests were positive. He offered to take me to the health clinic and 'handle it.' I couldn't believe he'd think that that would be okay in any kind of way! First of all, I assumed they'd contact my mom, since I was a minor. And then having to deal with all the protesters that've been in front of the women's centers lately. But the main thing, it went against my personal beliefs to go through with it. I truly thought Jester cared about me. But then he ghosted me several days before the shooting."

"He bailed." Astrid said.

"In a big way."

"So, when you confided in your former BFF that Jester had knocked you up, Britney acted like she supported you, but she was sizzling with rage, at both you and Jester. Naturally when Cassie comes along and tells her about the prank, she was gonna be all in. They'd planned to take out you and Jester as a revenge move. But leading up to that morning of the shooting? Jester started sweet talking Britney again, but when Cassie got wind, she wasn't having any part of it. She was furious when Britney told her. There you were, Jes, in the bathroom that morning puking your guts out, and Britney was frantically texting you to get to The Morgue. She wanted you and Jester there so Cassie would take you out. Cassie was ready to shoot all three of y'all, but no way would Britney have known she was a target too."

Astrid pulled her phone out from under her cushion and played the audio she'd made in The Morgue. There it all was. Cassie turning on Britney and shooting her, before and after she went after other kids. Shot after shot. The moment when Cassie told Astrid to run for her life and when she had, Cassie immobilized her. Jester screaming out for his sister and Cassie telling him she'd shoot him in the head if he made one move toward Astrid. An eerie moment of silence when not one kid was crying out for help, or moving, or weeping. Dead silence, as in the silence of the dead. Then, only a lone hiccup of tears - Jester's. The audio provided evidence that Britney had decided Jester had to go even if she hadn't said it outright, but Cassie's cryptic prattling told the story, especially the revelation that Jester had taken Cassie's virginity days prior. And had blabbed it to his friends. Had made fun of her.

Jes's audible gasp at the disclosure could be heard. And Cassie saying, "Our boy gets around, doesn't he, Jesamean? Brit told me about you and Jester and your big preggo problem. But I didn't know about that when Jesse called me and said he wanted to make it right between us, about what went down on Halloween."

Jester's sniffling ceased, along with some sort of shuffling caught on the audio, maybe Cassie shifting closer or Jester trying to inch away. Then Cassie's voice growing stronger when she said, "You took me on a legit date, didn't you, Jester Ray? You opened the car door for me and everything, smiling and ordering that foodie stuff you and Jes like, this nice restaurant I'd never been able to afford unless being treated. You smelled *so* good, and those gorgeous eyes of yours, grayish-green with amber, like sunshine bouncing off ocean waves, and when you asked if I wanted to finish what we started at Tish's party, I told you, yes. And we went to your mom's house because you told me she wouldn't be back for hours. You kissed me and took off my clothes, and you were so gentle, and it didn't hurt as bad as I thought it would, and when it was over, you acted so nice to me, Jester! You told me how much you enjoyed it and that we'd go out again soon and you hugged me hard at my door. But it was a lie. All of it."

There was Jes's voice on the recording, misty with tears when she cried, "Jester, is this true?! You've blown me off to carry on with Cassie? Knowing I've been desperate to talk to you!"

"I swear it's the truth," Cassie said. "And I'm pretty sure Jester boned Paloma the other day too, not that he's gonna admit to it now, huh, Jesse JR?"

"Everything, everyone I set up, was for the pranks," Jester says faintly, not admitting to doing it with Paloma, though his lack of protest bolstered Cassie's claim. "To up my social cred."

"So was mine and school royalty," Cassie said. "Until it wasn't. Until I knew I'd use the ruse to get back at all of y'all."

"I can't believe he did this with you! That he did me this way!" Jes cried. "After I've given all my love to you, Jester!"

"Jester loves no one but himself. And maybe Astrid, his bros, his spot on the prank scoreboard. Oh, and his dick," Cassie said.

Jester said something inaudible, maybe mumbling, or defending himself, but it was lost in the echo of The

Morgue. But Cassie's voice rang loud when she said, "Does all this make you want me to put him down, Jes?"

"Yes," Jes blurted, her affective ambivalence bubbling up.

"Do you really mean that?" Cassie's voice pitched, incredulous.

"I dunno. No. Perhaps."

"Please!" Jester cried, but exactly what he was asking for was not clear.

"Jester, go to your sister," Cassie ordered.

"What?"

"Go over by Astrid. *Now!*"

"Don't!" Jes cried, but whether she directed it to Jester or Cassie was unknown. Then, *dat-dat*! And a dull *thump* on the audio as Jester fell beside his sibling.

"Problem fixed," Cassie said. "And now, you can do something for me, Jes."

The recording went on between the two girls; more talk about how Jester had betrayed them. The audio captured the thirty seconds before Jes killed Cassie – because she had begged her to.

"You and Britney both didn't want to stop Cassie. You wanted her to take Jester out," Astrid accused.

"I didn't!"

"Your voice right there, Jes!"

"No, I never said for Cassie to kill Jester!"

"Y'all were talking about how he wronged the both of you!"

Jes gave Astrid a strange look.

"I was in shock, at everything that had taken place that day. I was trying to appease Cassie. I didn't say anything to encourage her! I never said what she did was okay!"

"A good prosecutor would poke holes in that, don't you think?"

Jes's brain felt like it would explode with all this information. Jes *had* seen red when Cassie revealed about her and Jester. Didn't mean she wanted him gone, did it?

"You think anyone's gonna let you run PEER if they heard this? That the college that gave you the four-year scholarship, is going to do that for someone who influenced a school shooter to kill her boyfriend?" Astrid said.

"It wasn't like that! Cassie had already made up her mind about Jester! And I'm doing so much good as the spokesperson for PEER," Jes's voice wobbled with anxiety. "I have to have this free ride to college, Astrid! To support my child. Your niece."

"You don't deserve jack!"

"So, you're going to tell everyone?"

"No. You are," Astrid said.

"I'll be raked over the coals! I won't even be able to get a low minimum-wage job! The scholarship is all I have left!"

"Have you told your mom about the baby yet?"

"No." But Jes wouldn't be able to hide it much longer. Despite keeping her weight down, her belly was beginning to protrude.

"Don't even think of milking my parents for money, not after you and your BFF's antics."

"Have you seen me asking? But don't you think they'd want to know their son's child?"

Astrid's laugh turned bitter. "Right. The murderess who wanted their son dead." They stared at one another. Finally, Astrid said, "I hear you won't be back at Manatee High this year. You plan to do online classes until your senior year. Then you'll move away to start college. That's an out for you. Maybe you and your mom should do that sooner."

"I'm starting a new PEER campaign this month. I'm gonna tell my mom about the baby then. And then we'll decide what's next."

"You think PEER wants a preg spokesperson? An unmarried Homecoming Queen?" Astrid asked.

"It's not the dark ages," Jes retorted.

"Still, some people only want people with old fashioned values. Ethics. Not girls who have sex with a guy who's doing other girls. Not someone who condemns tyrants but conspires with outcasts to kill people."

Jes stood. "I hope everything turns out okay for you, Astrid." She hid her trembling hands behind her back.

"Oh, I always make lemonade out of lemons."

"So…we're good?"

Astrid's laugh sounded like a canine bark. "Good? No, not good, Jes. By the way, better check your scholarship about a morals clause. While I'm not ratting you out about what happened between you and Cassie, the college might not be so cool with a knocked-up recipient."

"I'm giving back to the community, Astrid. Can't you see that?"

"Bullied girl fights for the bullied. Brava, Jes. You're giving back to yourself."

The thought poked. "Is there a time limit on your blackmail?"

"Like we're old and gray and it's still hanging over your head? Like you'll be sweating bullets — no pun intended, every day wondering if I'll post something on social. Naw. Won't have to. You know that I know, and that's enough for me. But karma, honey. I believe you'll be your own undoing," Astrid warned.

Jes left without another word, her shirt drenched with anxiety as she slid into the driver's seat, her belly rubbing against the steering wheel. No, she couldn't keep this a secret much longer. She only hoped Astrid could bear secrets for a lifetime.

CHAPTER THIRTY

An eagle-eyed journalist who'd followed the aftermath of the Manatee High School massacre ousted Jes's pregnancy, not Astrid. The journalist noticed Jes's expanding rounded stomach in recent months and delved into her past, uncovering Jes's relationship with Jester Pynes, a senior who had sadly died that fateful November day.

Several months after a school shooting in Middletown, Ohio and several weeks after the school shooting in Antiago, Wisconsin, in a packed public PEER meeting, several participants fired questions at Jes with raised voices and clouded expressions, venting their frustrations over the lack of progress in preventing school shootings. Standing confidently behind a row of microphones, Jes implored their continued support, presenting herself as their relentless agent of change.

A journalist asked point blank about the impending birth of her child. Several conservative PEER members gasped at the unmarried Jes. Her mother, who had come to cheer her on, turned pasty, blinking at her. Jes's cheeks filled with crimson, and she redirected the conversation back to the purpose of the meeting. But whispers continued to buzz like mosquitoes, leaving Jes wondering if she could sue the journalist for exposing her secret. However, she reasoned that if it was truth, then it couldn't be considered defamation.

As the meeting concluded, the usual requests for selfies with the hero or friendly questions were replaced by silence as the crowd parted ways. The ride home with her mom was not silent, as Jes's mother grilled her, and Jes admitted she was nearing the end of the last trimester of her pregnancy. Initially shocked, her mom eventually thawed like ice in a frying pan. The surprise quickly turned into excitement as they discussed plans and preparations.

However, as Jes's belly ballooned and Florida racked up more mass shootings, sponsors began grumbling and threatening to withdraw their support from PEER. Jes had crammed several years of high school into just a few months to get her GED, and now all she wanted to do was fast track her scholarship and relocate near the university that had awarded it.

Astrid's enigmatic postings on IG and FB about heroes and school shooters gnawed at Jes, causing her pregnancy heartburn to flare up like a raging wildfire. Astrid had assured Jes that she wouldn't reveal her secret, but just as the journalist had figured out Jes's pregnancy, what if someone connected the dots between Jes, Brit, and Cassie? What if someone believed she had influenced Cassie into shooting Jester? Innocent people faced accusations and wrongful convictions daily, a reality that chilled Jes. The recording Astrid had captured in The Morgue added to her unease. Anyone could exploit the subtle nuances to frame Jes in a sinister plot. The thought tore at her, the potential for twisting her words into an accusation.

Jes was going to become a mother, and she couldn't take those chances.

It was those very words she uttered to Astrid when she unexpectedly showed up at her house. Jes begged Astrid to hand over Jester's phone. However, Astrid responded with an acidic laugh, triggering Jes's tears as she began ransacking Astrid's room in search of the device. A tussle ensued between the pregnant Jes and the paralyzed Astrid.

As they gasped and strained against each other, Astrid's wheelchair tipped over, and her head thudded against her heavy oak desk. Blood poured from Astrid's head; she pleaded for help.

"Give me Jester's phone. Give me your phone."

"Jes! I'm really hurt. I think I have a concussion. My head is killing me!"

"Give me the phones!"

Astrid grunted as she tried to pull herself up, slamming back down to the ground. Blood continued to spurt from her head. Her tone faint, Astrid said: "Jester's. In the pocket of my rose-colored Valentino gown. Mine, top drawer beside my bed. Please tell the EMTs to hurry."

Once Jes had both phones in her possession, she told Astrid, "You know I can't help you, right? Especially now."

"I wasn't going to tell anyone, Jes. I didn't tell anyone about the baby, did I?"

"No. You just dropped hints all over the place. You posted GIFs that put me in a bad light. Sooner or later, someone's going to put that together. Is that what you wanted, Astrid? Your niece to grow up without her mother? Me possibly in prison, accused of conspiracy, my daughter raised by my mom instead of me?"

"I just wanted my brother to be alive."

"I didn't kill him!"

"No, you didn't. But you made sure that he'd be done in."

"And you made sure, just like all the other Blonde Squaders, Elites, and school royalty that people like Cassie would be tortured."

"Says the chick who ended up with the best-looking guy in school, but only after the top tiers got her there, along with Britney."

"You and Paloma got the glory for fixing up the losers. It elevated y'all's position, didn't it? But now, you're just as pathetic as we were."

"No good deed goes unpunished, does it, Jes?"

"It wasn't a good deed to benefit Britney and me. It was for everyone to see how the school royals ruled. But your crown has lost its shine."

"Are you going to call for help now? You got what you wanted. Please call 911! I'm hurting so bad!"

The blood gushed from Astrid's scalp, her legs entangled beneath the wheelchair. Jes gasped as sharp pains pierced her ribcage when the baby kicked, alarmed at her mom's jarring wrestling, and labored breathing. At that moment Jes realized she had to protect her daughter. No one could jeopardize their future, not even the child's aunt.

"I can't help you, Astrid. I have to save myself and my baby."

"You can do both, Jes. But if you leave me now like this, the gloves are off. I'll expose everything."

"No, you won't."

"Just watch me, Jes!"

"I'm sorry, Astrid."

"For what?"

"For this." Jes maneuvered the wheelchair over Astrid's fallen body and, summoning all her remaining strength, driving it over Astrid's neck. Once, twice, three times, ignoring Astrid's screams. Jes's breathing came in short bursts by the time she staged Astrid's tumble from her wheelchair, positioning Astrid's bloody head toward the desk but under the casters and her legs pretzeled up beneath the wheelchair. Astrid's deceased crumpled body was still warm to the touch as Jes mustered the strength to leave, despite dying to pee and the baby sitting on her bladder but not wanting to take the extra time there. She had to get away before Astrid's parents returned. She looked down at the surgical gloves she had put on during the conversation, not questioning why she had brought them or whether it meant that she had intended to kill Astrid anyway.

Jes managed to drive herself home, sobbing hysterically in the car, her bladder threatening to burst. Astrid's family had lost one child, now they had lost another. It was cruel and horrible, but Jes believed that her child had to live at the expense of Astrid's life.

Jes and her mother had packed up all their stuff and were moving to the university town where Jes would attend college. Having completed all her high school courses/GED requirements, Jes's college would allow her early entrance into the scholarship program. Jes would not only be attending college but also head up the PEER program at the local high school campus nearby. A nationally recognized platform has ensured the position now comes with a salary. Additionally, Jes's current OB had recommended another doctor in the university town who would deliver Jes's daughter in a few weeks.

Jes knew she would never be suspected of Astrid's death. After all, the move had been planned for weeks. Jes had tossed both phones, together with the surgical gloves, into the bay on her way home, that horrible day she ended her friend's life. Astrid's death would simply be considered an unfortunate mishap. Another tragedy stemming from the aftermath of the Manatee High School massacre. Just another one.

However, a nagging thought plagued Jes. What had she overlooked? What if Astrid had made a copy of the audio from The Morgue? No, she shook it off.

Everything would be fine. She'd go to college, earn a degree, continue with PEER, and raise her daughter.

Astrid's parents' anguished wails reverberated through the house when they stumbled upon their daughter's crumbled body. EMTs arrived on the scene, and their expressions were grim as they delivered the pronouncement. Detectives followed suit, their investigation uncovering no signs of foul play. Astrid appeared to have tumbled from her wheelchair, her head striking the desk with a sickening thud. In a desperate attempt to rise, her legs, unresponsive and numb, became ensnared beneath the wheelchair, her neck twisted in the process. The coroner's verdict, albeit tragic, painted a picture of an accident, not a sinister act. Astrid's room offered no incriminating clues pointing to homicide.

So, had Jes got away with murder, literally, as she embarked upon her new life with her unborn daughter and her mother? Did actions have consequences or only when they were discovered? Was Jes complicit in the murders of Jester and eventually, cleverly, of Cassie, or was she the hero of the hour? Only Astrid knew and Astrid was dead. But the tiny camera, embedded into a locked desk drawer in the dead girl's room had, unknown to everyone - except perhaps Astrid, and maybe that was why she had asked Jes over, so that the camera she knew was there would record the conversation she and Jes would have and would reveal that Jes's actions had not been without their own brand of malice and revenge. Embedded in the Morgue's recordings were the searing exchanges between Cassie and Jes, and Jester. Jester, Jesse JR, the boy whose transgressions had ensnared their lives and who had been confronted by the harrowing price of his recklessness - the barrel of a loaded gun, aimed at him when Jes granted implied permission, and Cassie delivered the kill shot. Would the secrets held within this camera ever be revealed? Would Jes's callous killing of Astrid, also caught in the relentless lens of the tiny hidden camera ever be played back or would Astrid be laid to rest and her secrets with her.

Another victim of the Manatee High School shooting.

Just another one.

ABOUT THE AUTHOR

Just Another One is not D.C. Rivera's first novel, although it is her debut for Provoco. An established author of dark and chilling novels for older teens and young adults, D.C. blends a unique writing style with a macabre design to delve deeper into the darker side of teenage and young adult psyche, exploring emotions that most teenagers keep well hidden.

Her writing is often raw and startlingly realistic. The subject matter of Just Another One, a high school shooting, is brave and disturbing as revelations about the shooter and the reasons for the shooting are revealed.